MW00902882

FROM BLUES TO SMILES TO JOY

FROM BLUES TO SMILES TO JOY

How to Have a Great Day Every Day

Alan Phillip, C.P.

Passionist Community Press
Sierra Madre, California
with **Spirit of Hope Publishing**
Irvine, California

FROM BLUES TO SMILES TO JOY: *How to Have a Great Day Every Day*
Copyright © 2011, Alan Phillip, C.P.
Published by Passionist Community Press
with Spirit of Hope Publishing

International Standard Book Number: 978-1-929753-37-6
Printed in the United States of America

Written by Alan Phillip
Edited by Jerry Seiden
Cover Photos by Alan Phillip
Inside Photos by Alan Phillip

ALL RIGHTS RESERVED: No part of this publication may be reproduced, stored in a retrieval system, or transmitted in any form or by any means—electronic, mechanical, photocopying, recording, or otherwise—without prior written permission, except for brief quotations in critical reviews or articles.

Scripture texts in this work are taken from the New American Bible with Revised New Testament and Revised Psalms ©1991, 1986, 1970 Confraternity of Christian Doctrine, Washington, D.C. and are used by permission of the copyright owner. All Rights Reserved. No part of the New American Bible may be reproduced in any form without permission in writing from the copyright owner.

NOTE: This book is designed to provide information on the subject matter covered. It is provided with the understanding that the publisher and author are not engaged in rendering individualized professional services. If medical advice or other expert assistance is required, the services of a competent professional should be sought. The checklists in this book are not designed to substitute for professional evaluations or psychotherapy.

The anecdotal illustrations and personal stories in this book are composites of real situations or personal recollections in which facts may have been altered, liberties taken, and/or names changed to protect the privacy of certain individuals.

For information or permission contact:
   Spirit of Hope Publishing
   PO Box 53642
   Irvine, CA 92619-3642

   Phone: 714-308-2494
   Email: info@spiritofhopepublishing.com
   Web: http://www.SpiritofHopePublishing.com

Dedication

To Fr. Thomas More Newbold, C.P.
My mentor for many years.
I owe him much.

Acknowledgements

I want to thank Mr. Glen Golden, Mrs. Nancy McKenna, and Fr. Peter Berendt, C.P., for carefully proof-reading the manuscript and offering their corrections and suggestions. I also want to thank Mr. Jerry Seiden of *Spirit of Hope Publishing* for mentoring me through this book project and skillfully improving the text and layout.

Table of Contents

CHAPTER	TITLE	PAGE

BACKMATTER

Become a possibilitarian.
No matter how dark things seem to be or actually are,
raise your sights and see possibilities—
always see them for they're always there.
—Norman Vincent Peale

Introduction

It's Monday. You sit, stare out the window and watch the drizzling rain. A frown fixes itself on your face as you go through a bout of melancholy. You munch on a piece of chocolate, but it doesn't help.

It's Saturday night and you don't have a date. Another lonely evening looms ahead. You go through a few rounds of self-doubt and the blues. You reach for the phone and call a friend. No answer.

It's late at night and you can't sleep. You don't know exactly why but you are crying.

You start counting sheep. The sheep fall asleep, but you don't. You start wondering if anyone really cares.

Do rainy days and Mondays get you down? Do the blues and the blahs come calling more often now than before? Is there an underlying sadness in your life, even though most things are going well? Are there days when you have no motivation and just want to stay in bed until noon? Are you dejected, forlorn, glum, pessimistic, and in an emotional recession? Do you wish you felt happier and more energetic? Then this book is for you. This book addresses the common human experience of feeling "down in the dumps," or what I call "mild temporary depression." The ideas and suggestions in this book are meant to help you get through the gloom and feel better tomorrow.

I am a Catholic priest. In forty-five years of ministry I have worked with people suffering from all types of depression. This book puts into practical format many of the common sense things that I have learned. Although I recommend that you read the book from beginning to end, on any given day you may want to check the <u>Table of</u>

<u>Contents</u> and read a chapter that you think tackles a root cause of your feelings. The <u>Check List</u> at the end of the book serves as a handy reminder of suggested actions to take.

Feelings of depression can stem from hundreds of sources. This book will discuss a number of the more common psychological, emotional, and spiritual causes.

First, consider the following important questions:

- Is your depression heavy and constant?
- Do you wrestle with despair?
- Do you have feelings of worthlessness and thoughts of suicide?
- Have you had a string of sleepless nights or do you sleep too much?
- Have you had long crying spells?
- Is it difficult to concentrate or make decisions?
- Do you blame yourself and feel that the negative events around you are all your fault?
- Do you have severe headaches, chronic fatigue, poor appetite, or panic?

A yes to half or more the questions above may indicate a "clinical depression." This is beyond the scope of this book.

It is estimated that twelve million Americans are afflicted with serious depression. The following link has more on clinical depression and an online test: <u>http://psych.med.nyu.edu/patient-care/depression-screening-test</u>. Please note that this is only a preliminary screening test for depressive symptoms. It does not replace a formal psychiatric evaluation.

Another helpful resource is the *International Foundation for Depressive Illnesses.* See: <u>www.ifred.org</u>.

Also check out the *Depression and Bipolar Support Alliance* at www.dbsalliance.org. This site provides a confidential online mood disorder screening evaluation. The site also has information about local support groups.

The *National Institute of Mental Health* is another resource for information and help. Visit their site at: www.nimh.nih.gov. For immediate help go to: www.nimh.nih.gov/health/topics/suicide-prevention/if-you-are-in-crisis-and-need-immediate-help.shtml.

Freedom From Fear also offers helpful resources: http://www.freedomfromfear.com/links.asp.

For anyone with thoughts of suicide or the urge to harm yourself call 1-800-784-2433, now. It is a nationwide 24 hour, 7 day a week helpline—staffed by people who are care. To find a local number see: http://suicidehotlines.com/.

For both mild as well as serious depression, the first step is to get a physical examination. Many forms of depression are the result of physical conditions like hypoglycemia (low blood sugar), diabetes, weak adrenal function, an under-active thyroid and environmental allergies. You may also have a hormone imbalance, a chronic infection or a vitamin deficiency. Another contributor to depression can be the regular use of over the counter and prescription drugs. If you are taking any drugs on a regular basis, ask your doctor or pharmacist about the side effects.

If your depression has a physical cause, your doctor may prescribe an anti-depressant. He may also recommend some dietary and life-style changes.

If your depression is heavy and constant even after following your medical doctor's advice, your next step is to seek out a good psychiatrist or psychotherapist. With the right kind of professional help, a person with clinical depression can learn how to cope better and get back into enjoying life. Help and hope *is* available.

Did you hear about the preacher who dreamt he was giving a sermon? He awoke to find his congregation seated before him!

I have yet to fall asleep during one of my sermons or homilies, but I must admit I have seen people in the congregation nodding now and then. They say that one effective way to keep listeners from dozing off is to follow this format:

1. Be clear.
2. Be brief.
3. Be gone.

Following that advice, the chapters in this book are short and to the point. I have tried to crunch a lot of information into a few pages. I have also borrowed from the wisdom of many people, sprinkling their words throughout the book. In fact, this book can be described as a tapestry, with thoughts and reflections woven around meaningful quotes. The bottom border of this tapestry is made up of references to books and websites. Because each chapter is meant to stand alone, you will find some repetition in the book. Some quotes will appear more than once.

In writing about thirty ways to deal with common depression, I do not imply that this is a comprehensive and complete treatment. It is a beginning. These brief chapters are meant to open the doors for further reading, reflection and processing. The chapter on anger, for instance, will not in three pages cure many years of seething resentment. But each chapter offers a practical starting point. And the references to books and websites at the end of the chapters will point you to further resources for the healing journey.

The first edition of this book was titled *From Blues to*

Smiles. It had twenty four chapters, but only three centered on a faith perspective. This revision is titled *From Blues to Smiles to Joy.* Each chapter brings in values from the Christian faith. I believe that the many behavioral and psychological tools available to us can bring us smiles. But true and lasting joy is found only through Christ.

So, for those of you who are having a "down in the mouth" day, I offer to you this faith-filled journey into joy.

—Fr. Alan Phillip, C.P.
Sierra Madre, California

Chapter 1

Coping with the Blues
The Basics

For you have been purchased at a price.
Therefore glorify God in your body.
—1 Corinthians 6:20

When someone comes for counseling and tells me that he is depressed, it is important for me to discern how the serious the depression is. I ask him to describe what he is going through. If it sounds like deep, ongoing, clinical depression, I refer him to someone more competent than myself. If their problem is perceived as temporary mild depression, I prepare myself to work with him.

In either case, my first duty is to ask him, "Do you want to get better?" He might be startled and respond, "What?" So I ask again, "Do you really want to get better, to get completely rid of your depression?" I hope he says, "Yes, that's why I am here." But he may hesitate to answer my question. Why would *anyone* hesitate? Depression is not fun. And, whether mild or serious, most people would want to get rid of depression, right? Not necessarily.

Believe it or not, there are some people who feel good about feeling bad. They might not be conscious of it, but they find some pleasure in feeling down.

First of all, depression gets them attention. People around them say, "Oh, you look so down. You poor dear. I feel so sorry for you. It must be awful what you are going through.

Tell me all about how difficult your life is."

Secondly, depression gets them out of work and relieves them of a lot of responsibility. When they are down and out, other people will not turn to them for assistance. Instead, others say, "Oh, I'll do this task. I can see you aren't up to doing anything right now."

In order to get well, a person must want to get well. I mean, *really* want to get well. They must be determined and fully committed to do whatever it takes to get well. That means they must be willing to spend whatever time it will take, make whatever effort is necessary, call upon whatever resources are available to them, outlay whatever cash is required and, if they are a person of faith, do constant prayer work in order to get well.

If a hypochondriac comes to a doctor for a cure but doesn't *really* want to get well, nothing the doctor prescribes will work. As a counselor I am willing to do all I can for a counselee. But if the counselee is not totally committed to getting rid of their depression, I ask them not to waste my time. Nothing I do will work for them.

When a person with everyday mild depression says they are **committed** to getting well, we are off and running.

I go into my five starting questions:
1) Do you get enough **sleep**?
2) Do you eat **balanced meals**?
3) How much weekly **exercise** do you get?
4) How much do you **play**?
5) Are you getting enough **light**?

These questions are so obvious that I am almost embarrassed to ask them. But dealing with these fundamental issues up front often alleviates much of the problem.

1) Sleep

As long as I can remember, doctors have said that the average person requires eight hours of **sleep** to be healthy and function properly. Nevertheless, many of us are so busy that we tend to cut back on sleep whenever we can. We try to sneak by with less than eight hours. We justify cutting back on sleep because we have so much work to do.

To motivate ourselves to get enough sleep, it helps to remember that sleep deprivation eventually diminishes the effectiveness of our actions. Our reflexes are not as sharp. We tend to make stupid decisions. We are less alert when driving. We may say dumb things that we would not say if we more alert. And sleep deprivation eventually affects our mood. We get cranky and crabby. We feel drained, drowsy, and all done in.

Guess what the solution is? Doctors say to get eight hours, or close to it. That's the first step in combating depression.[1]

2) Balanced Meals

Eating **balanced meals** is more in the category of "Mother says...." In my case, it was my mother, grandmother, and older sister. I was a fun-loving kid who just wanted to go outside and play. I didn't want to lose playtime by stopping to eat. Fortunately, my dear mother "forced" me to sit down and eat. And since she was from the farm, she knew what a balanced meal consisted of. I grew up healthy and, with good eating habits, have remained healthy. Thanks, Mom.

I have a popular knowledge about nutrition, but am not qualified to give any in-depth advice. Books on good nutrition fill local libraries and bookstores, plus there is a plethora of information available in magazines and on the internet. All of us need to read and keep abreast with the latest discoveries about how to stay healthy. A firm commitment to our physical well-being begins with a firm commitment to be informed.

For a rule of thumb: No one puts cheap fuel in a Mercedes. Our body is much more precious than a luxury car. We need to treat our body with utmost loving care. We need to provide it with the highest quality and right amount of nutrition. Our body will give us many years of loving service in return.[2][3]

3) Exercise

Doctors, mothers, and just about everyone nowadays will tell you about the importance of **exercise**. It is good not only for physical health, but also for mood elevation, mental alertness, improved digestion, better sleep, greater energy and a sense of accomplishment. Exercise also contributes to longevity.

My mother was physically healthy and mentally alert well into her eighties, in part because she never drove a car! She walked—to the store, to the bank, to church, to the bus stop and, when she wanted to go to downtown Chicago, she walked six blocks to the train. Did I say Chicago? For fifty years she lived in a suburb of Chicago, so that means she often walked in rain, sleet, snow, and *wind*. What a lady!

> *A vigorous five-mile walk will do more good for*
> *an unhappy but otherwise healthy adult than all*
> *the medicine and psychology in the world.*
> —Dr. Paul Dudley White

Getting motivated for exercise is a challenge for many people. They know exercise is important. But they tell themselves, "I'll do it next week." My advice: find exercise that you enjoy doing. Many people enjoy walking. Others prefer jogging, biking, swimming, golf, etc. One of my earlier forms of exercise was roller-skating. Accompanied by good music, I could skate for hours. Gardening does it for others.

Many people live in cold climates where it is difficult to spend time outdoors much of the year. With no access to a gym, indoor health club, or skating rink, what can they do? Walking around a Mall is a possibility, if a Mall is accessible. Calisthenics is usually possible at home, but for some this is not enjoyable. I recommend music. Play a favorite selection and then dance or "dancercise" to the music.

Another strategy is to pretend you are directing an orchestra. This can be a great upper-body workout. If I were rich enough and had the space I would buy a drum set. Have you ever seen an over-weight drummer? What a happy way to stay fit! The trick is to be creative and find an enjoyable way to work out. Any brisk, rhythmic exercise for at least thirty minutes releases molecules in the brain called endorphins, which quickly work to wipe out anxiety and depression and boost self esteem.[4][5]

> *Above all do not lose your desire to walk. Every day I walk myself into a state of well-being and walk away from every illness. I have walked myself into my best thoughts, and I know of no thought so burdensome that one cannot walk away from it.*
> —Soren Kierkegaard

4) Play

One of the first rules of thumb that we were taught as kids was: *All work and no **play** make Jack a dull boy.* Without play, Jack is not only dull, but also depressed.

Play has the power to resurrect the child within us and thereby reduce the size of adult problems. Play is a great equalizer, bringing together people of all ages, colors and creeds. Play diminishes our possessiveness of material things, encouraging us to share so that others may join in our play. Play helps us gain perspective. Play is an act of freedom.

> *Your mental health will be better if you have*
> *lots of fun outside of that office.*
> —Dr. William Menninger

> *People who cannot find time for*
> *recreation are obliged sooner or*
> *later to find time for illness.*
> —John Wanamaker

Most Americans don't feel valuable unless they are useful and productive. So we work and work in order to produce and produce. We need to balance work with play. Putting fun and relaxation into our day refreshes our spirits and renews our energy. Play is ultimately productive, for it leads to a healthier and more creative life.[6][7]

The rules are simple:
1. Grab your hat.
2. Grab your coat.
3. Leave your worries on our doorstep.
4. Just direct your feet to the playful side of the street.

> *The life without festival is a*
> *long road without an inn.*
> —Democritus (400 B.C.)

5) Light
Finally, **light.** Growing up in Chicago, I know how crabby people can get by the time the month of March rolls around. The result of a long, cold winter is called "cabin fever" or

"winter blues." It is estimated that 10% to 20% of our population goes through some form of this. (A more serious illness afflicting 4% to 6% of Americans is called Seasonal Affective disorder, SAD.)[8] This is the result of having to spend so much time indoors.

Natural light deprivation leads to depression. Darkness contributes to depression. Because sunlight appears to stimulate the production of melatonin, which influences our mood, proper emotional maintenance involves going outdoors every day. Also, all rooms except our bedroom during sleeping hours should be well lit, with bright colors, cheerful pictures, and window curtains opened wide. Full spectrum lighting, which produces light similar to that of the sun, is recommended.[9]

To sum up: In order to progress from blues to smiles to joy, the first step is **Commitment.** Then we need to take stock and see if we are getting enough:

1. **Sleep**
2. **Nutrition**
3. **Exercise**
4. **Play**
5. **Light**

In Matthew 19:19, Jesus tells us, "You are to love your neighbor as yourself." Implied in this statement is the obligation to love ourselves. Getting a good night's sleep, eating balanced meals, making time for physical exercise, and enjoying play and light are all part of caring for ourselves.

These strategies are a basic plan for dealing with depression. But more, they ar part of the foundation for a healthy spiritual life. St. Thomas Aquinas reminds us that "grace builds upon nature." If we neglect the legitimate needs of our human nature, our spiritual efforts will have no foundation to build upon. We will be building on air.

End of Basic Course, #101.
Let's go on to the rest of the lessons.

Chapter 2

Accept Reality

Sufficient for a day is its own evil.
—Matthew 6:34

$\mathcal{H}$ow well I remember my childhood days of reading fairy tales, watching cartoons and sitting through western movies. Every story had a conflict. Once the conflict was resolved, the final statement was trumpeted, "And they lived happily ever after." For a while I expected that my life would someday turn into "happily ever after." It didn't take long before I realized that this just wasn't going to happen. In fact, quite the opposite. I soon learned the cynical wisdom of Murphy's Law,* "Whatever can go wrong will go wrong."

*If you cheer for the Chicago Cubs as I do, you know that Murphy's Law is known as the *Wrigley Field Law.*

I believe in bad luck.
I believe I will always have it,
and I plan accordingly.
—Napoleon Bonaparte

A fundamental strategy for coping with depression is to expect it. Expect a lot of things to go wrong in life and expect to feel lousy from time to time. This may seem like obvious advice, but not everyone is willing to accept it. They somehow believe that the world owes them a good time, and that life is somehow unjust if they fall into bad luck.

We waste a lot of time and energy trying to deny or run away from pain. If we meet it head on, we stand a good chance of dealing with it successfully. A wise father once advised his constantly complaining daughter, "My dear, if you would just accept the fact that life is difficult, it would be so much easier."

> *Life is difficult. This is a great truth, one of the greatest truths. It is a great truth because once we truly see this truth, we transcend it. Once we truly know that life is difficult—once we truly understand and accept it—then life is no longer difficult. Because once it is accepted, the fact that life is difficult no longer matters.*
> —M. Scott Peck

Introductory Depression

Depression will come in various shapes and sizes, depending on our life situation. Early on in life, we can expect **"Introductory Depression."** This is the sadness and misery we experience when we receive a poor report card, don't make the team, aren't chosen homecoming queen, or don't get the date we want for the prom. Every young person has a long list of these.

Physically-Caused Depression

There is **"Physically-Caused Depression."** This is the beat-up feeling that follows after an operation, after giving birth, during menopause, or the rotten mood we are in because we didn't get enough sleep or we have a toothache that won't go away

Passage Depression

There is **"Passage Depression."** This is the emotional pain we go through when we have to let go of a section of our life. It comes about when we are leaving home for the first time, moving out of an old neighborhood, walking our daughter down the aisle, retiring from a job, etc. This also results when we realize our abilities are diminishing. We don't have the energy we once had. Our memory is not what it used to be. We can't hit the golf ball as far as we did last year. We dread the reality that we are getting older.

The Blues

The most poignant depression comes when a relationship goes sour. This is labeled **"The Blues."** If we risk getting involved in dating and allow our self to fall in love, there is the gloom and doom feeling if we lose out. She or he no longer loves us and now wants out of the relationship. If we enter the challenging relationship of marriage, we may be among those who suffer through the devastation of a divorce. Heartache seldom gets any worse than that.

Most blues songs center around a relationship failure in one form or another. At times it is good for us to listen to these songs, enter into them, feel the feeling, and let the words name our experience as best they can. Tears have a cathartic affect.

Parenthood is another risky and challenging relationship. It's wise to prepare for the rebellion stage that children will go through. Teens will say mean things, question our decisions and disobey our commands. Sometimes our children may reject us completely and go off the deep end as far as the values we hold. Yes, being a parent makes us vulnerable to a host of wounds. We may feel like a total failure and question why we even became a parent in the first place. We can sink into self-doubt and fear.

Bereavement Depression

There is **"Bereavement Depression."** Anybody who has ever lost a loved one knows what this feels like. It is very difficult to let go of a parent, spouse, child or close friend. Their death in some way diminishes us. The most devastating sorrow comes when someone we love commits suicide. Not only is there a great shock at the loss. There is the gnawing sense of guilt or blame, followed by a lifetime of wondering if there was something we should have said or done. This is a tough one.

Disappointment Depression

I like to include a catchall category called **"Disappointment Depression."** This is a frequent occurrence. We try to lose weight but don't, so we get frustrated. We forget where we put our house keys, so we feel stupid. We try a new moneymaking idea and it doesn't work, so we feel foolish. We make a wrong turn and get lost, so we begin thinking we're losing our mind. We may dent someone's car in a parking lot, forget to pay a bill, drop a vase, burn the roast or show up for an appointment on the wrong day. This list grows with each passing day.

World View Depression

Finally, there is **"World View Depression."** This is the result of watching or reading too much news. So many terrible things are happening in our town, in our country, and in our world. There is war, terrorism, oppression, poverty, hunger, injustice, homelessness.... the list goes on and on. Any person with even half a heart is bound to get depressed when exposed to so much suffering and pain in our human family. We not only feel bad for those who are hurting, but we also feel frustrated because of our inability to alleviate their situation.

Compassion

Imagine this cartoon: Charlie Brown puts down five cents at Lucy's booth to pay for her counseling help. Lucy advises, "Adversity builds character. Without adversity a person can never mature and face up to all the things in life." Charlie asks, "What things?" Lucy responds, "More adversity."

One real plus to personal adversity is that our tears of sadness and depression help us understand what others go through. We can knock on any door in any neighborhood and we will find there an individual or a family who has just had, is having, or will soon have some serious suffering. Of all the gifts of the heart, the one most needed today is the gift of **compassion.**

Compassion is the ability to understand another's pain and by our presence help them carry their burden. To appreciate what another person is suffering binds us to them, links us to their human experience and gives us an entry into understanding. Unity of the human family will come about, not when everyone shares a common spoken language, but when everyone recognizes the universal vernacular of tears.

No one seeks out physical pain, emotional distress or depression. But these negative experiences remind us that we are alive, that we have feelings and that we are genuine human persons who can hurt and bleed. Interestingly enough, it has been noted that the nerve endings that bring on our tears are the same nerve endings that give us feelings of happiness. The more we drink of the cup of sorrow, the more our emotions are capable of joy. Walking through dark valleys enables us to scale loftier heights.

Time

Our experiences of depression teach us what a friend we have in **time.** All things pass. The most exciting victories will soon be diminished memories. And the most consuming sorrows will one day be vague recollections. Yes, time heals. Time gives our soul the space it needs to deny or reject, then feel, accept, get back on our feet and walk forward with our head held high. When a bout with depression hits us, we can say, "I was expecting this. I've gotten through this before and I'll get through it again." As a famous singer crooned, "Life goes on, and this old world keeps right on turning."

Love

As for relationships that are on hold, going sour or gone under, I find consolation in a line from the movie, *The Other Side of the Mountain.* At one point in the story there was a parting scene. A young couple very much in love had to be separated for a long period of time. The man uttered this sentence which I never forgot. "How **lucky** is that person who loves someone so much that it is so difficult to say 'goodbye'." If we have never felt that lucky, it may mean that we are a rock or an island. We feel no pain. Nothing could be sadder.

> *Life is made up of sobs, sniffles, and smiles,*
> *with sniffles predominating.*
> —O. Henry

Preparation

Expecting some troubles and expecting some degree of depression gets us ready to cope with whatever life throws at us. This was the insight of a dear friend of mine named Millie. Millie was born without any legs and spent her entire life in a wheelchair. She not only learned how to adjust to her physical problems, but she also came to understand the inevitability of human suffering. As a school secretary and registrar she came into contact with a lot of troubled people, and was the unofficial counselor to many of them. One day she reflected, "Everyone is handicapped. Mine is just more visible."

> *Although the world is full of suffering,*
> *It is also full of the overcoming of it.*
> —Helen Keller

Make Pearls

I propose that we take the oyster as a role model. When a grain of sand works its way inside the shell of an oyster, the oyster moves into action. It starts to reduce the irritation by coating the sand with layers of soft, iridescent mother-of pearl material from its shell. Little by little the oyster transforms the painful irritation into a beautiful pearl of great value. That's what Helen Keller did to her blindness and deafness. We can do the same when depression hits us. See it as a grain of sand in our way. Attack it, transform it, and go on.

One of the most poignant scenes in the gospels is that of Mary, the mother of Jesus, holding the dead body of her son in her arms on Calvary. This event inspired the great *Pieta* sculpture of Michelangelo. Many painters have tried to capture on canvas this moment of pain. It is not difficult to imagine the agony that Mary suffered at that moment. Yet I believe she also possessed an inner hope. Mary knew what St. Paul was to write later to the Romans, "We know that **all things work for good** for those who love God..." (Romans 8:28). In the midst of her grief, Mary knew that somehow God would draw good out of all the evil that was happening. Mary waited. Mary hoped. And Easter happened!

I don't know how or where or when. But the same God who brought Israel out of slavery in Egypt to freedom in the Promised Land, the same God who raised Jesus from the dead on Easter morning, this same God can raise us up from failure to success, from suffering to joy, and from death to life. That's how God works. That's where his power shines.

> *Even though I walk through a dark valley,*
> *I fear no harm for you are at my side;*
> *your rod and staff give me courage.*
> —Psalm 23:4

Beautiful thoughts blossom into a beautiful life.
Bad thoughts grow into weeds.
You are your own gardener.
Your tool is your mind.

Chapter 3

Take Charge of Your Thoughts

Whatever is just, whatever is pure,
whatever is lovely, whatever is gracious,
if there is any excellence and if there is
anything worthy of praise,
think about these things.
—Philippians 4:8

We've all seen the bumper sticker that says, "Think Peace." I like the one that says, "Forget peace. Think about using your left turn signal!" These bumper stickers remind us of a most basic psychological law.

In the second century Marcus Aurelius Antonius noted, "Our life is what our thoughts make it."

Virgil agreed, "They are able because they think they are able."[1]

Norman Vincent Peale stated," Change your thoughts and you change your world."

This truth is echoed in the Constitution of the United Nations' Educational, Scientific and Cultural Organization (1946), "Since wars begin in the minds of men, it is in the minds of men that the defenses of peace must be constructed."[2]

You are today where your thoughts have
brought you; you will be tomorrow
where your thoughts take you.
—James Allen

There is a transforming power in our thoughts. Thoughts focus our attention. Thoughts place a goal before our eyes. Thoughts mobilize our energy. After that, our bodies and emotions spring into action.

Yes, as the bumper sticker declares, if we think peace, we will get peace. If we think war, we will get war. If we envision success, we will get success. If our thoughts dwell on failure, we will get failure. If we think happy thoughts, we will get happy. If we think gloomy thoughts, we will get depressed. Garbage in, garbage out. Diamonds in, diamonds out. The choice is ours.

> *We have the tool of thought within us to*
> *create a thousand joys or a thousand ills.*
> —James Allen

"You say that the choice is mine? But how can I control my gloomy thoughts? They just seem to come. I always look at the dark side of life." Answer: *Passing* thoughts come to all of us. We seem to have little control for what passes quickly in and out of our minds. But *dwelling* thoughts... These are our responsibility. Our wills make a choice about what our minds *dwell* upon.

When doom-and-gloom thoughts want to set up shop in our head, we have to throw them out. We tell ourselves, "I am not going there." "I am going to take charge of my thoughts." "I *choose* not to think about that." Because our minds don't like to be blank, we must be prepared to divert our attention and refocus our thoughts in another direction. It helps to keep some interesting thoughts ready in the wings, like planning a task that we are excited about, reflecting on a hobby that requires our concentration, or imagining a faraway place we would like to travel to.

*The greatest revolution of our generation is
the discovery that human beings, by changing
the inner attitude of their minds, can change
the outer aspects of their lives.*
—William James

Negative Self-Talk

Let's start with **negative self-talk.** A lot of the conversation buzzing about in our head is conversation with our self. What do we say to our self?

Many people engage in negative self-talk about their body. "I am too heavy." "I am too skinny." "I have too much acne." "I've got too many wrinkles." "My nose is too big." And on and on goes the disapproving inner dialogue.

Young people are especially self-conscious about their looks. They also worry about failure to measure up in class, in sports or socially. Their negative self-talk leads to a Charlie Brown complex. They wonder if anyone likes them. "I am such a klutz." "How could I be so stupid?" "I will never amount to much." "I can't accomplish this goal." "I am a failure." "I have so few friends." They are filled with self-doubt.

As people get older and start to lose some abilities, they too began to put themselves down. "I am so clumsy." "I am so forgetful." "I just don't seem to get much done."

Then there is the devastating self-talk called comparison. "Why can't I be like so-and-so?" "I wish I were smarter, or more athletic, or better looking, or more successful like so many others." Next we might throw in some guilt talk. "I shouldn't have done that." "I wish I didn't say that."

On and on go all the harmful, unconstructive, pessimistic and disapproving thoughts that push us deeper and deeper into depression. As we go about feeling bad about ourselves, along comes a joker who agrees with some of our harmful self-talk. This makes us feel even worse.

Sometimes we repeat the negative tapes programmed into our heads by our parents, teachers, other adults, or peers from our childhood. Do we want them to have such power over us? I propose that we blast away at negative self-talk and not believe what we hear. Let's not give these thoughts the time of day. They are wasting our valuable time and energy.

Positive Self-Talk

Let's replace life draining self-talk with **positive self-talk.** Let's proclaim the truth about ourselves. For example:

- I am a worthwhile human being.
- I am a child of the universe and I deserve to be here.
- I am a beautiful person.
- I like people.
- There is no one quite like me anywhere.
- Without me the world would lack someone very unique.
- I am in the image and likeness of God.
- I like me.
- If I have hurt anyone, I am sorry.
- I am doing better now.
- I have learned a lot and I continue to grow.
- My patience will win over my pain.
- I have done a great deal of good and I will do much more.
- Nobody can be me but me.
- I can do it.

The poet, Peter McWilliams, gave this sage advice: "Increasing your self-esteem is easy. You simply do good things and remember that you did them." Without a doubt, we have all done many, many good things. Positive self-talk begins with remembering these good deeds, thinking about them, feeling good about them and, with Tom Thumb, saying to our self, "What a good person am I!"

When we are feeling disheartened and depressed, we can use a psychological trick on ourselves—*act as if*. First, visualize what we would look like if we were happy, confident, and feeling good about ourselves. Then proceed to "act as if" we are such a person. Even though initially we are acting on the outside, this will affect both our inner thoughts and emotions until the "act" becomes a reality.

A key ingredient here is to smile—even if it's forced. The mere shape of the muscles from ear to ear will change our emotions from head to toe. Then think, *What a beautiful day! How great to be alive. I want to jump for joy and kiss the sun. Hi, world. I'm here and I want to be here.*

Wow, I can walk, talk, dance, and sing! This is going to be a great day for everyone I meet. I am going to make them happy.

OTHER CAUSES OF NEGATIVE THINKING

Here are other causes of negative thinking we need to look at:

People

We need to walk away from those toxic people who are always complaining, criticizing, judging and whining. We don't need them in your life, especially if we are the intended victim of their stinging remarks. Instead, we can choose to hang around with positive people, people with smiles on their faces and sunshine in their hearts. Observe little children. They are full of wonder and it is contagious.

News

I suggest that we read or listen to the news sparingly. So much of it deals with negative events, not upbeat happenings. If the newspaper headlines are depressing, turn to the comic section. When the news comes on the TV, turn to the Discovery Channel. When your computer flashes a news bulletin, don't click for the rest of the story. It is important to stay informed about major issues, but most of us could do without all the details.

Music

There is cruelty and trash talk in many modern songs. I advise that we choose wisely what we listen to. Hearing or singing the "blues" can be cathartic for a time, but a steady diet can feed depression. We need to find music that has a happy beat, upbeat lyrics and inspirational thoughts. We need to soak in music that is just plain fun. Playing a musical instrument is another way to bring joy into our souls. Dancing sounds will work their way into dancing thoughts.

Self-Censorship

We need to realize the power we have of controlling what goes into our minds and what our minds dwell on. We need to teach our children the art of self-censorship. The media and the market place will throw at us whatever sells a product. If a TV program is banal, switch channels. If a movie is offensive, walk out. If a magazine is pornographic, don't buy it.

We have the ability to choose what we watch or listen to. We have the ability to choose what we think about and what stays in our thoughts. By our words and by our actions, people will know what is on our minds. Mean thoughts lead to mean words and destructive actions. Positive thoughts lead to positive words and constructive actions.[2]

The happiness of your life depends upon the quality of your thoughts: therefore, guard accordingly, and take care that you entertain no notions unsuitable to virtue and reasonable nature.

—Marcus Aurelius Antonius

Once we get negative thoughts out of our way, we are ready for making positive contributions to life. We are ready to put the power of thought into all sorts of creative directions.

The ancient Egyptians thought, "Ah, pyramids." And today people still gaze upon these wonders of the ancient world.

Michelangelo thought, "Ah, a likeness of David," and out of a block of marble came a majestic statue.

Alexandre Gustave Eiffel thought, "Ah, a tower." And out of a pile of steel a Paris landmark was built.

Charles Dickens thought, "Ah, a story about greed and goodness." His popular *Christmas Carol* still fascinates us during the holiday season.

There is no work of art, architecture, literature or music that was not first of all a thought.

Bible Balancing Act

Bible reading requires a balancing act. There are passages that remind us of our littleness, and meditating on these words can help us grow in humility. There are passages that remind us of our sinfulness, and reflecting on these words can lead us to deeper repentance. But we need to experience the full biblical perspective by reading those passages that point to our goodness and greatness in the eyes of our Creator. I suggest we take some time, contemplate the following words, and feel the arms of God wrapped around us.

> In the book of Deuteronomy, we are told that that God was guarding his people as "the apple of his eye" (Deuteronomy 32:10).

> God says to his people in the book of the prophet Isaiah, "You are precious in my eyes" (Isaiah 43:4). And again in the book of Isaiah, God says, "You shall be called my delight" (Isaiah 62:4).

> In the book of the prophet Zephaniah, we have these uplifting words, "God will rejoice over you with gladness...He will sing joyfully because of you, as one sings at festivals" (Zephaniah 3:17-18).

> St. Paul informs us that "while we were yet sinners, Christ died for us" (Romans 5:8). In other words, even though we are imperfect, God loves us.

> Later St. Paul reminds us, "Do you now know that you are the temple of God... that temple is holy" (1 Corinthians 3: 16-17).

We need to receive these words with open ears and believe in our inner goodness put there by God. Then we have to give ourselves some positive self-talk. *Hmmm... I am God's beautiful creation, and the apple of God's eye. God rejoices over me. I am a holy temple.*

Reflecting on these truths can lead us to proclaim with Mary, "He who is mighty has done great things for me. Holy is his name" (Luke 1:49).

A Jamaican grandfather was talking to his grandson about his inner turmoil. He confided, "I feel as if I have two wolves fighting in my heart. One wolf is the vengeful, angry, violent one. The other wolf is the loving, forgiving, compassionate one." The grandson asked him, "Which wolf will win the fight, Grandpa?" The grandpa paused for a moment, then said, "The one I feed."

Thoughts are like food. If we choose to stuff our head with negative thoughts, we can expect a destructive and depressing life. If we dine on positive thoughts, we can expect a creative and joyful life. Each day the choice is ours.

> *Good thoughts bear good fruit, bad thoughts*
> *bear bad fruit—and man is his own gardener.*
> —James Allen

Chapter 4

Talk to or Communicate with Someone

I will speak in the anguish of my spirit;
I will complain in the bitterness of my soul.
—Job 7:11

Common sense tells us that when we are depressed, the first action step is to talk to someone. Anyone. Ideally, we should be able to talk to someone in our family—spouse, parents, brothers or sisters.

If our family is not available or is part of our problem, turn to friends. If our family and friends are not around, that's the time to turn to someone in our church community, a fellow worker, our barber or hairdresser—anybody who is willing to listen. It is essential for us to communicate our thoughts and feelings to another human being when we are emotionally down.

Sometimes it is hard to admit that we are having trouble and that we need other people. But everyone needs somebody sometime. Everyone. Nothing can substitute for human contact. Often we will discover that talking to another is all that was needed to change our mood. Once we start explaining, sharing, venting and feeling understood, we know that we are no longer facing our problems alone. A burden has been lifted or at least made lighter. We discover new power to carry on. Even if the other doesn't completely understand us, the fact that they are willing to listen gives us strength, courage and hope.

Trouble is a part of your life, and if you don't share it, you don't give the person who loves you a chance to love you enough.
—Dinah Shore

Putting words to our feelings helps us identify and clarify what's going on inside us. If we have confused thoughts, talking gives us time to analyze them, sort them out, and make some sense out of them. If we are physically uptight, talking can relax our muscles. If we have pent up emotions, talking can set them free.

If we can't find words to describe what's going on inside us, it is acceptable to express ourselves non-verbally—by crying, beating our pillow, or humming a sad song. The important thing is to identify and not deny what we are feeling and then communicate it to another human being. After coming to grips with reality, we will be equipped to take the necessary action steps. "Ah.... It doesn't feel so bad now. I can handle this."

The world is so empty if one thinks only of mountains, rivers and cities. But to know someone who thinks and feels with us, and who, though distant is close to us in spirit, this makes the earth for us an inhabited garden.
—Johann Wolfgang von Goethe

Where do we start? We grab a phone and call someone in our family. We take a friend out to dinner. We write a letter or email someone whom we can confide in. Even a text message or a chat room communication may serve our immediate need for connect. We should be forthright with the other person. "I need to talk to you. Do you have a few minutes?" Perhaps after talking with someone we know, it may become clear that we could use the help of a professional counselor or therapist.

In the past people felt embarrassed to go to a counselor. They felt it was a sign of weakness or mental illness. That was unfortunate. If we have a toothache that won't go away, it is smart to go to a dentist. If we have a heartache that we can't shake off, it's a sign of strength and wisdom to turn to another for help.

Not everyone is proficient in face-to-face conversation. Some people stumble with spoken words and feel they can't express themselves accurately. Others saturate the air with words as a way of dodging their feelings and thoughts. Talk therapy has its limitations. I suggest we use every means available to communicate to another what it is that we are going through.

Journal

Some people keep a **journal** of their feelings and then share the journal with a friend. Journal keeping allows us to underline, use exclamation points, and mark the text with arrows and other markings to emphasize our thoughts as we write. Putting our experience in writing helps us clarify what we are going through. When we share our writing with another, they have more time to ponder our words and comprehend our pain.

Drawing

Others may be more comfortable **drawing**. Drawing enables us to illustrate our moods on paper with various colors and strokes, or draw a symbol that reflects our state of being. A sketch of a cloudy day, a dark cave or a withered flower may be all we need to tell someone what we are going through. (If we are dealing with children who are feeling sad, drawing is a very effective way for them to communicate with us.)

Music

A powerful tool of communication is **music**. Those who play an instrument may perform a melody that conveys their disposition. For those who sing there are a multitude of songs that express soul-searching and heartache. Some may attempt an interpretive dance to let out their feelings.

> *(Music therapy) can make the difference between withdrawal and awareness, between isolation and interaction, between chronic pain and comfort—between demoralization and dignity.*
> —Barbara Crowe[1]

Literature

Good **literature** can give us the words we need to connect us with our emotions. Then we are able to share our feelings with another. Read an appropriate poem or recite dialogue from a novel or play and bring what's on the inside out.

> *I believe that a poem is a window that hangs between two or more human beings who otherwise live in darkened rooms.*
> —Stephen Dobyns

Rituals

Doing **rituals** in the presence of a sympathetic friend is another way of expressing a deep level of soul. For instance, burying a picture (loss of a loved one), planting a tree (new beginning), breaking bread together (reconciliation), lighting a candle (sign of wisdom acquired), throwing a tattered pair of shoes into a pond (getting rid of old angers), attaching a bandage over one's heart (healing), or placing bread and wine upon an altar (waiting for transformation) are all symbolic actions to communicate that we are letting go and starting anew.

The bottom line is this: When we feel depressed, we need to talk to—communicate with—someone and let him or her help us carry our pain. Then some day in the future, we will be able to listen to, share in, and help someone else carry their pain. That's how life works. It's beautiful.

> *Come to me all you who labor and are*
> *burdened, and I will give you rest.*
> —Matthew 11:28

These words of Jesus encourage us to present all our problems to God in **prayer**. When we can't find anyone else around to listen to us, the Lord is always present. A person of faith will often turn to prayer before seeking out a human person to speak to. We need not go into great detail about our problems, for the Lord already knows what we are enduring. We simply let go and let the Lord take over.

> *Cast all your worries upon him*
> *because he cares for you.*
> —1 Peter 5:7

Chapter 5

Listen

*She had a sister named Mary who sat beside
the Lord at his feet listening to him speak.*
—Luke 10:39

Did you hear about the lady who went to lawyer and requested help with a divorce?

The lawyer asked her, "What are your grounds?"

"Oh", she said, "we have about an acre and a half."

"I mean," the lawyer said, "do you have a grudge?"

"Oh, yes," she replied. "We have a two car garage."

"Lady," the lawyer tried again, "does your husband beat you up?"

"No," she said. "I usually get up an hour before he does."

Finally the exasperated lawyer asks her, "Do you want a divorce or not?"

"No," she answered, "I don't want a divorce. My husband does. He says we can't communicate."

Has this ever happened to you? You announce to a friend that you just had a car accident and that you will have to replace a fender. The friend responds, "Oh, that's nothing. Let me tell you about the accident I once had."

Your friend starts regaling you with her tale of woe before you have a chance to finish yours. In fact what you wanted to talk about was your fear of getting into the car and driving again. But you never got around to that part of your story.

Have you ever attempted to inform your husband about an argument you had with a neighbor? Before you get to the part about your feelings, your spouse responds, "Aw, don't worry about it. I never liked her anyway. You're better off not even talking to her." What you wanted to tell your spouse was that the argument resurrected an unhealed memory of your mother, but he wasn't poised to listen any further.

> *A man is already halfway in love with*
> *any woman who listens to him.*
> —Brendan Francis

When we try to communicate something that is deeply personal and important to us, we want the other to listen and understand. But if they are distracted and not paying attention, if they quickly dismiss our feelings before we fully express them, or if they are more concerned about what they will say next, the result is frustration. We failed to connect with their heart. Loneliness follows. And we get depressed.[1]

Listening

In the book, *Seven Habits of Highly Successful People*, the author Steven Covey identifies **listening** as one of those habits. He tells a story about a salesman who, despite his best efforts, was about to lose a sale. In his final effort, he switched tactics. Instead of giving his eloquent sales pitch, he tried listening intently to the words of the potential customer. The salesman would nod when he understood and ask questions when he didn't, totally and sincerely focused on the needs and concerns of the one speaking. It worked. The client felt his needs were understood. The sale went through.[2]

The first duty of love is to listen.
—Paul Tillich

Listening is an art, the art of seeing into another's soul. Like any successful artist, a successful listener must engage in discipline and hard work.

Discipline

The **discipline** involves a very limited use of the word "I." We have to put aside our need to talk. We have to choose not to interrupt, argue or compete for attention. We have to be careful not to jump in, assuming we know what the other is thinking before he or she tells us. We have to be patient because some people speak in circles, and it takes a while before they express themselves clearly.

Hard Work

The **hard work** involves giving the other person our full and complete attention. This means staying alert. This means listening with our ears and hearing every word. It means listening with our eyes and catching the non-verbal communication signals the other is employing. It means listening with our emotional sensors, picking up the depth of feeling being conveyed. It means listening with our intelligence, to the connotations and denotations of expressions, striving to grasp the meaning of the other's words, actions and emotions. It means listening with our heart, not judging, but being aware of the importance of who the other is.

It is love that prompts us to honor another person with our total concentration. We have to communicate by our demeanor (e.g. put down the newspaper or the cell phone and look them in the eye) that we consider him or her worth listening to.

> *The greatest gift you can give another*
> *is the purity of your attention.*
> —Richard Moss

Well-Primed

Like any worthwhile human endeavor, it is important to come to a listening situation **well-primed**. The handy priming "tool" I use is a slip of paper that I carry in my wallet. On this paper I have typed twelve sentences or phrases for possible use when responding to another in conversation.

"Tell me more."
"You must feel...."
"It sounds as if...."
"You've been going through a lot, haven't you?"
"You mean to tell me...."
"You sound upset."
"Did I hear you correctly? Did you say...."
"I'll bet that was... (awful, wonderful, fun, or tiring)."
"I didn't realize that you felt that way."
"If I understand you, you...."
"That's interesting. Go on."
"Wow!"

It takes skill to paraphrase what another has said. It takes effort to relay back to them what we think we heard. But accurate feedback, accompanied by appropriate nods, quizzical looks and timely questions are the tools of attentive conversation. We will know we have succeeded in the art of listening when the other proclaims, "Oh, thank goodness, you understand!"

Listening is the most powerful force we know for releasing potential in others. Real communication occurs when we listen with understanding—to see the idea and attitude from the other person's point of view, to sense how it feels to them, to achieve their frame of reference in regard to the thing they are talking about.
—Carl Rogers, Psychologist

Our world is a noisy world. TV's and radios are blaring. Neon signs are flashing. Billboards are glaring. Cell phones are ringing. Everyone wants us to tune in to their message: "Buy this." "Vote for that." "Do this." "Go to that." Words bombard us from every side and we end up hearing nothing. Is it possible to mute the external noise, create for our self some inner peace and prepare the ears of our hearts? What will happen if we do?

When we listen to nature, we learn the lessons it is reaching out to give us. When we listen to ourselves, we come to discover new horizons of possibilities. When we listen to others, we grow to understand, appreciate, and celebrate their richness. And when we listen to nature, ourselves and others, we stand a good chance of tuning in to the mind and heart of God.

I want to sit and listen and have someone talk, tell me things—their life histories— books they have read, things they have done—new worlds! Not to say anything—to listen and listen and be taught.
—Anne Morrow Lindbergh

In the opening quote of this chapter we recalled how Mary listened at the feet of Jesus. The Lord tells Martha (and us) that Mary has "chosen the better part." When we pray, it is the "better part" if we keep our words brief, and spend a lot more time listening.

When we take the time to listen to the Lord, we may hear the **unsettling** news that life is not about us. When we are in pain, it is so easy to get all wrapped up in our own little world. But there is a bigger picture. As Pierre Teilhard de Chardin, said, "Something is afoot in the universe." We are but a speck of dust in a vast cosmic reality. It puts our few years of pain on earth in an eternal perspective.

When we take the time to listen to the Lord, we may hear the **comforting** news that our suffering has infinite worth. Through baptism, we become one with Christ. Therefore, in some mysterious way our suffering becomes his suffering. Is our body racked with pain? Jesus says, "This is my body." Are we bleeding? Jesus says, "This is my blood." And Jesus does not suffer in vain. His suffering has eternal value. Somehow our small Calvary is linked to his great Calvary and our lives take on a dimension of meaning we never imagined. Hearing that message gives us a rock foundation for joy.

Chapter 6

Manage Anger

*The Lord is gracious and merciful, slow to
anger and abounding in love.*
—Psalm 145:8

Were you irritated the time someone cut you off in traffic? Were you upset when you got punished in school for something you didn't do? Did you get annoyed when you were passed over for a promotion at work? Did your blood boil when someone insulted your race, religion, or your country? Perhaps you were outraged when someone cheated you. Perhaps you became infuriated when someone harassed your spouse. Maybe you got into a heated argument and almost started a fight? Yes, we have all gotten angry and mad at one time or another.

Anger is energy. The challenge we face is how to manage this anger energy. Failure to deal with anger appropriately can lead to violent acts. Failure to deal with anger appropriately can waste an extremely powerful force for good.

Admit
Timing is everything. It is very important that we **admit** to ourselves when we are angry. "I am upset. I am very upset. In fact, I am fuming." To deny the experience of anger, to put it off, to not face it or to bury it causes the anger energy to turn inward. We transfer the anger on to ourselves, perhaps even feeling that we are the guilty party. If anger is not dealt with, it will go under, fester, and find its way back

into our life, eroding our self-esteem and dragging us into a sulking gloom.

Identify

After we admit to anger, the next step is to **identify it.** We should be specific. "I am angry that the driver cut me off in traffic." "I am upset that my friend lied to me." "I am irritated that my employee didn't do the job right." "I am mad that my daughter did not do her homework." "I am upset that my husband did not clean up the garage." It is helpful to verbalize out loud what it is that is making us mad. Hearing our own voice identifying the content of the anger will help us judge how serious it is or isn't.

Communicate

Next, it is important that we **communicate** our feelings. We need to report to the other person or persons involved what we are going through. We can inform them, "I am angry, upset, irritated, and mad because of what you said/did." However, what we communicate is our emotions only. We should not attack the personality or integrity of the other person. We should not insult them, call them names, make obscene gestures or swear at them. We should not judge their motives, their intentions or their state of awareness at the time of the incident. And we should not give them the silent treatment, which is another form of mismanaged anger.

It is enough to just inform the other what we are feeling. Then we should give them an opportunity to respond. Perhaps they will correct their words, apologize for their actions or promise to do better. For us to insult them or judge them cuts off communication, solves nothing, and leaves us still wallowing in our anger.

I was angry with my friend; I told my wrath,
my wrath did end. I was angry with my foe;
I told it not, my wrath did grow.
—William Blake

A common problem on our highways is road rage. A driver cuts in front of us, or fails to yield, or is on a cell phone and doesn't notice the green light and we blow up. Don't these drivers know that we are in a hurry?!? Often our anger is understandable. The other person does something illegal or stupid.

Ager at the Action
However, rather than curse the person, I suggest we direct our **anger at the action**. The action they did was wrong. We are angry because we have a keen sense of what is right and wrong. So we acknowledge that we are justifiably upset.

The next step is to say a prayer for the offending driver. We don't know what may be going on inside the driver's head. Maybe he just lost his job or received a bad report from his doctor. Perhaps a loved one recently died or maybe he had an argument with his wife. We don't know. If we direct our anger at the action and say a prayer for the person, our emotions will be vented correctly. And we will end up spending a lot more time talking to the Lord.

Anger dwells only in the bosom of fools.
—Albert Einstein

Write a Letter
Some practical advice about managing anger comes from Abraham Lincoln. One day the President's Secretary of War, Edwin Stanton, was having trouble with a major general. It seems this general insulted him and accused him of favoritism. Stanton brought this up to Lincoln who suggested

that he **write a letter** to the general and express his anger.

Stanton did so. Then he showed his livid letter to the President. Lincoln was impressed with the powerful language. He asked, "What are you going to do with this letter?"

Surprised by the question, Stanton replied, "Send it."

Lincoln shook his head. "You don't want to send this letter. Put it in the oven. That's what I do when I have written a letter while I am angry. It is a good letter. You had a good time writing it and feel better. Now, burn it and write another."

Act

The next-to-final step is to **act** appropriately. We might want to ask for an apology, call for a change of behavior, negotiate a compromise or fire the offending person.

The key here is to let the weight of the event, not the intensity of the feeling, dictate our actions. We may be very upset about not having the morning paper delivered on time. The intensity of our feeling may be caused by our battle with insomnia the night before. Reflecting on the event may help us realize that missing the paper is no big deal. So we decide not to fire the paperboy or kick the dog.

> *Violence is the last refuge*
> *of the incompetent.*
> —Isaac Asimov

Let Go

Finally, it is imperative that we **let go.** A group of scientists set out to capture a particular species of monkeys in Africa. They wanted to bring the monkeys back alive and unharmed. But they had to catch them first.

The scientists made traps that consisted of small jars with long, narrow necks. They placed a handful of nuts in each jar. Then they waited. When the monkeys eyed the scene, they thrust their paws into the long neck of the bottle and grabbed a handful of nuts. As they tried to withdraw the nuts, the monkeys noticed that their clinched fists would not pass through the narrow neck. But they were unwilling to let go of their prize. So, dragging the bottles around, the monkeys were easily taken captive.

Anger is like that. If we hold on to anger and refuse to let it go, we carry a burden with part of ourselves trapped inside. We carry a trap of our own making. Wisdom tells us to let go of the anger. Let it go!

The bottom line is simple. If anger energy is misdirected, negative things happen. If anger energy is appropriately directed, positive things happen. The choice is ours: to tear down and destroy, or to build up and give life.

"Do you mean that anger can be constructive and give life?" Here are some examples:

Anger grew in the soul of Moses when he saw his people bound in slavery. This anger spurred him on to demand of the Egyptian Pharaoh, "Let my people go" (Exodus 5:1). The determined Moses proceeded to lead his people out of slavery to freedom.

Anger at unjust practices and policies energized the American colonists to stage the Boston Tea Party. King George and Parliament weren't moved. The colonists' anger grew, led to the Declaration of Independence, and gave birth to a new nation.

It was anger at racial prejudice that strengthened Martin Luther King, Jr. to stand up, speak out, and resist non-violently the social inequality in our country. It cost him his life but not before he launched a new era of freedom and justice.

These people identified their anger, communicated it eloquently and channeled it into constructive action.

Anybody can become angry—that's easy; but to be angry with the right person and to the right degree, and at the right time, and for the right purpose, and in the right way—that is not within everybody's power and is not easy.
—Aristotle

Reader's Digest often prints articles entitled, *That's Outrageous!* These articles tell horror stories about the abuse of power, the misuse of tax dollars, the outlandish interpretation of laws, etc. The magazine runs these stories in hopes of making enough people like you and me angry. This anger will motivate us to act appropriately, that is, to change the system, speak out for new policies and elect better officials.

A person who does not know how to be angry does not know how to be good.
—Henry Ward Beecher

Look around the world today. What do we see that gets us upset? Where are the laws unjust, the people oppressed and the forces of bigotry in control? Where is the situation unfair and the use of money and power out of balance? Where is the environment abused? Where are human life and human dignity threatened?

Imagine what would happen if the same anger-power that eliminates innocent people in wars could be turned toward eliminating hunger. Imagine what would happen if the same anger-energy that leads to street violence could be channeled toward providing cleaner streets and better sanitation in poor countries. Imagine what would happen if the same anger-energy that develops into physical and verbal abuse in the home could be turned toward helping the homeless. Imagine what would happen if the same anger-energy that escalates into foul and abusive language could be converted toward abolishing illiteracy. Imagine....

> *In my pantheon of heroes the best of men are...*
> *spiritual warriors who are alive with moral*
> *outrage, and who enter the arena to wrestle with*
> *the mystery of evil in one of its many disguises.*
> *Fierce men, rich in considered judgment, who*
> *still have thunder and lightning in them.*
> —Sam Keen[1]

There was thunder in the voice and lightning in the eyes of Jesus when he drove the money-changers out of the temple. He was not afraid to take action. He admonished them, *"It is written: 'My house shall be a house of prayer,' but you are making it a den of thieves"* (Matthew 21:13). And those who were buying and selling in the temple hightailed it out of there. They could see the moral outrage of Jesus.

The saints speak about seeking union with the Lord in his suffering. It is also holy to seek union with the Lord in his anger. Any wrong that would upset Jesus should upset us.

> *A person is as big as the things*
> *that make him or her angry.*
> —Winston Churchill

When our anger is just, we become energized to take positive action. Then at the end of our days, we will stand tall and feel good about ourselves. We will know we made a difference for a better world in our lifetime.

Chapter 7

Conquer Fear

Do not be afraid. Go on speaking,
and do not be silent, for I am with you.
—Acts 18:9-10

One of the most common causes of unhappiness is regret...

...If only I had said.
...If only I had acted.
...If only I had not held back.
...Oh, what might have been?

The culprit is fear. We wanted to speak out but were afraid of what others might say. We wanted to take action but were afraid that others might make fun of us. We wanted to take advantage of an opportunity but were afraid we might not succeed. We wanted to act but were afraid to try something different. We were controlled by fear—fear of being unpopular, fear of losing power or prestige, fear of failure, fear of change, fear of getting hurt, and fear of venturing into the unknown. So now we wallow in regret. And that leads to an ongoing sadness.

For of all sad words of tongue or pen, the
saddest are these, 'It might have been.'
—John Greenleaf Whittier

Is there something from our past that we are still regretting because we were too afraid to speak or act? Maybe we were afraid to take the car keys away from our drunken friend before he or she went out and had an accident. Maybe we failed to own up to a mistake on the job and somebody else got fired. Maybe we were fearful of flunking and now regret not getting our degree.

If we are still feeling ashamed of events of the past, this negativity can drag us into a long siege of depression. We need to talk to someone about our regrets. (cf. Ch. 3) Then we need to bury these regrets. That's the past. The past is like school. We learn from it and then move on, smarter and wiser. Today is a new day. We have a fresh start and from this moment on we act with new resolve.

I had a dear old friend who died at the age of ninety-one. I used to joke that he didn't have to worry about peer pressure. All his peers were dead. If we let it, peer pressure can be very controlling. Some teenagers dress in a certain style or behave a certain way because of peer pressure. "Everybody's doing it." Some adults go along with dishonesty in a business venture and cave in to peer pressure. Some politicians vote against their conscience for fear of losing votes in the next election. Everyone has a desire to fit in and be accepted. But is it worth it, if it means compromising our principles and our integrity?

You can avoid the depression that results from regrets. Resolve each day to accept peer pressure from only one person—yourself. Know who you are and what you stand for. Know the kind of person you want to be and act accordingly. Let criticisms fall where they may (cf. Chapter 9). The sad outcome of conformity is this: everyone likes you, but you hate yourself. The fruit of courage? The pride of looking in a mirror and smiling at what you see. You like yourself, you love life, and you look forward to the future.

If Rosa Parks had taken a poll before she sat down in the bus in Montgomery, she'd still be standing.
—Mary Frances Berry

Here are a few *What Ifs....*

Mohandas Gandhi

Mohandas Gandhi didn't like the way the British government was running India. He felt his people were being treated unjustly. The British Government said, in effect, "Too bad, because that's how things are." *What if* Gandhi said, "All right, if that's the way you want it. I don't want to get into any trouble"

That's not what happened is it? Employing non-violent civil disobedience, Gandhi went about organizing peasants, farmers and urban laborers. He led nationwide campaigns for easing poverty, expanding women's rights, building religious and ethnic amity and increasing economic self-reliance. Gandhi was imprisoned for many years but eventually his efforts resulted in the independence of India from foreign domination.

Rosa Parks

Rosa Parks didn't like the indignity of having to sit in the back of a bus because of the color of her skin. The lawmakers and custom keepers of the time said, "Too bad, but that's the way things are." *What if* Rosa responded, "Well, if that's what you people want, I guess I'll go along. I don't want to upset anybody."

Fortunately, that isn't what she said. She spoke clearly and eloquently when she plunked herself down in a front seat of a bus in Montgomery, Alabama. There was a fire for justice in her soul, plus the courage to act. And from that act the civil rights movement took birth and proceeded to overturn centuries of official discrimination.

Alexander Solzhenitsyn

Alexander Solzhenitsyn didn't like the political oppression that was taking place in his country, the former Soviet Union. The political leaders told him, in effect, "Too bad, because that's how things are and are going to be." *What if* Solzhenitsyn responded, "All right. If that's the way you politicians want it, I'll adapt. I don't want to lose my income as a writer."

That's not what happened, is it? Solzhenitsyn continued to teach and write against the system. He was imprisoned and eventually deported. But there was a fire for human dignity in his heart along with the courage to act. Eventually, thanks to his bravery and that of many others, freedom triumphed with the downfall of Communism.

Michelangelo

What if Michelangelo had worried about criticism? What if he was frightened that he might fail in painting a ceiling? What if he decided to play it safe? Then, as one writer observed, tourists in Rome today would be gazing at the Sistine floor.

I like to read stories of courage, like that shown by Patrick Henry, Rosa Parks, and Alexander Solzhenitsyn and Michelangelo. Stories like these help stiffen our backbones for battles with fear.[1]

Courage

The dictionary defines courage as "that quality which enables one to pursue a course deemed right, through which one may incur contempt, disapproval, or opprobrium." It is encouraging to hear about people whose hearts are on fire for human rights, for the preservation of our environment, for the end of nuclear weapons, for the control of guns and for education reform.

Most of these are peace-loving people. But for them it is not peace at any price. They know that to take action often means the beginning of conflict and division. Some lose jobs and careers, some lose friends, and some even lose their lives. These people believe in an outer peace that comes from truth and justice. They believe that inner peace can only come by being faithful and true to oneself.

Life shrinks or expands in
proportion to one's courage.
—Anais Nin

It takes courage not only to stand up for what we believe. It takes courage to face loneliness. It takes courage to deal with suffering. It takes courage to admit when we are wrong and ask for forgiveness. It takes courage to forgive even when the other is not sorry. It takes courage to get up after we have failed. It takes courage to love, even though we know our hearts may break again.

Self-Esteem

Where does courage come from? Courage does not come from thin air. It has roots—deep roots. The first root is **self-esteem.** Self-esteem is a clear realization of who I am. It is an understanding of my own dignity and worth as a human being. This dignity and worth comes with creation and does not depend on what others think or say (cf. Chapter 8). To feel confident about who we are helps us face difficult situations with strength and daring.

Strong Conviction

The second root of courage is **strong conviction.** The founders of our country were keenly aware of the injustices imposed upon the colonies. These founders possessed moral outrage and a passion for setting things right. "We hold these truths..." They wrote out their beliefs in the Declaration of Independence and then they signed their names irrevocably in ink! Having deep-seated values and firm principles drives out fear and gives us the nerve for bold action.

Ability to Accept Change

The third root is the **ability to accept change** and deal with the resulting discomfort. You can't steal second base with your foot on first. You can't become a butterfly without saying goodbye to the comfort of the cocoon. You can't have the blessings of freedom without saying goodbye to old securities.

Determination

The fourth root is the **determination** to see our goal achieved. That means that our desire for a goal is so intense that we don't count the cost. That means we choose not only to talk the talk but also walk the talk—even *run* the talk. We are filled with enthusiasm and don't ever look back.

Self-esteem, strong convictions, ability to change, and determination are the solid foundations for courage. But when the going gets really tough and the opposition is formidable, something more is needed.

> Moses was asked by God to lead his people out of slavery in Egypt to freedom in the Promised Land. Moses felt inadequate. He even claimed that he was a poor speaker. Moses said to God, "Who am I that I should go to Pharaoh and lead the Israelites out of Egypt?" God answered, "I will be with you" (cf. Exodus 3:11).

Jeremiah was asked by God to be his prophet and proclaim his message to the people. Jeremiah protested, "Ah, Lord God, I know not how to speak. I am too young." The Lord answered, "I will be with you" (cf. Jeremiah 1:4-9).

Gideon was asked by the Lord to save Israel from the power of Midian. Gideon replied, "Please, Lord, how can I save Israel? My family is the lowest in Manasseh, and I am the most insignificant in my father's house." The Lord assured him, "I will be with you" (cf. Judges 6:14-16).

The apostles were directed by Jesus, "Go, make disciples of all nations" (Matthew 28:19). Earlier he has told them, "I am sending you like sheep among wolves" (Matthew 10:16). And, "If they persecuted me, they will also persecute you" (John 15:20). The apostles must have thought, "We are the ones who let you down on Calvary. We were too afraid to stand by you when you needed us. Who are we to go out to all nations?" Jesus reassured them, "I am with you always, until the end of the age" (Matthew 28:20).

If we get out of bed in the morning to face the day and we depend only upon our wisdom, our strength and our cleverness, we have good reason to be afraid. The wolves will prevail. But if we place our lives totally in the hands of God, trusting that his power and his love will be with us, we can sport an unflinching smile.

O Most High, when I am afraid,
in you I place my trust.
—Psalm 56:4

Who has power in our life? If we worry about what others think or say, we have given them power over us. They control us. We live our life trying to please them or live up to their expectations. It is like a prison. We are not free.

There is a Country and Western song that was out a few years ago, and its refrain is worth memorizing. "Life is not tried; it is merely survived, if you're living outside the fire." So let us ask ourselves, "What can we do, now that we are not afraid?" What a wide world of possibilities opens up, once we are free of fear!

Do you fear the force of the wind,
The slash of the rain?
Go face them and fight them,
Be savage again.
Go hungry and cold like the wolf,
Go wade like the crane;
The palms of your hands will thicken.
The skin of your cheek will tan.
You'll grow ragged and weary and swarthy.
But you'll walk like a man.
—Hamlin Garland

When we die, God is not going to ask us how well we conformed to others' image of what we should be. God will ask us if we were true to what he called us to be.

If you want to know the heart of a person,
watch how they treat animals and flowers.

Chapter 8

Know Your Inner Truth

*God looked upon everything he had made
and found it very good.*
—Genesis 1:31

There is a cartoon which shows the character Ziggy sitting on a psychiatrist's couch. The psychiatrist is giving his diagnosis. "Ziggy, you don't have an inferiority complex. You are simply inferior."[1]

Have you ever felt inferior, mediocre or second-rate? Do you compare yourself to others and feel you are not as smart, or as talented, or as successful as they are? Do you see more failures than successes in your life? Do you see yourself as falling short of your ideals and goals? Do you worry that you don't measure up to your parents' hopes and dreams? Do you see others as better looking than you? More popular? More deserving?

Do you dread the next class reunion because you haven't accomplished very much in your life? Do you frequently say to yourself, "I can't do it?" Chances are that these thoughts and feelings of inferiority have piled up and buried you under feelings of depression. Ah, that's a good starting point for a journey.

The journey I would like to take you on is a journey into your inner self. You have no map for this journey, so please keep your eyes, ears, mind, memory and heart open. I think you will like what you see. Although the words below won't take much time to read, to accomplish this journey may take weeks. Take your time.

First level, picture yourself as a creature of the earth, connected to it by air, water and food. Your days are governed by the sun and your years by the seasons. Then extend yourself to feel as a child of the universe, existing in time and space, subject to nature's laws, vibrating with energy, in rhythm with the universe and in sync with the sound of the heavens.

This initial stage of the journey involves looking around at obvious and easily observable aspects of yourself. Remember a time you made someone in your family happy. Think about some successes in school or on the job. Answer the questions: What kind of food do I like? What kind of music do I enjoy? What are/were my favorite subjects in school? What are my favorite sports? What are my hobbies? Where have I traveled to and where do I hope to travel to in the future?

A **second level** in this journey also involves remembering. When did you laugh the hardest? When did you cry the most? What are your biggest fears? What makes you angry? What are your regrets? What are your dreams? For what have you been forgiven? For what are you most thankful?

Now down to a **third level**. Just what is it that you stand for? What do you often speak about, teach or proclaim? What are the beliefs and values that guide your choices and decisions?

The **fourth level** is the treasure-house level. Here recall the people who are most important to you. Who do you think about the most? Who do you pray for most often? Who among the departed do you miss the most? Who do you enjoy the most? Whom would you be willing to die for?

The **fifth level** concerns integration. When are you most creative? When do you choose to be alone? Imagine the male and female aspects of your personality, the 'yang' and the 'yin'. How do you balance the diversity of talents and traits you have? If married, how do you compliment and fulfill your spouse?

The **sixth level** is enormous, mysterious and mostly unknown. It is the level lost from memory, the part of you that bubbles, groans and stirs about with all of your stored up experiences from the womb to the present moment. This is the subconscious. It is not our purpose to analyze this but to just acknowledge the presence of a vast reality that is unique to you.

The **seventh level and final destination** of the journey is the center of your being. Even before you get there, observe the light and feel the warmth. Notice the dazzling colors and the rapturous sounds. Sense the pulsating of your heart and the feeling of being fully alive. Behold—you have reached the inner core of your being, the source of your beauty, your goodness, your truth. This is a sacred place.

> *God created man in his image; in the divine image he created him; male and female he created them.*
> —Genesis 1:27

> *What are humans that you are mindful of them...You have made them little less than a god, crowned them with glory and honor.*
> —Psalm 8:5-6

> *Everything has beauty, but not everyone sees it.*
> —Confucius

> *I still believe in spite of everything that people are really good at heart.*
> —Anne Frank

> *Each person has inside a basic decency and goodness. If he listens to it and acts on it, he is giving a great deal of what it is the world needs most..., It takes courage for a person to listen to his own goodness and act on it.*
> —Pablo Casals

Some people have a difficult time believing the journey's end, that the center of their being is good and noble. Aware of all their faults and failings, they will acknowledge only a small portion of inner goodness. Although they may stand in wonder at the sights and sounds of nature, they are still blind to the interior world of the soul.

To affirm our inner worth is not to claim we are without faults. As long as we are living, we are a work in progress. The work we are about is releasing more and more of our core beauty, so that it permeates all our thoughts and actions

> *Everyone has inside himself a piece of good news.*
> *The good news is that you really don't know how*
> *great you can be, how much you can love, what*
> *you can accomplish and what your potential is.*
> *How can you top good news like that?*
> —Anne Frank

One summer while I was still in graduate studies, I had the opportunity to work at the Illinois State Penitentiary in Statesville, IL. This facility housed over three thousand prisoners. My job was to conduct interviews and collect information for the prison chaplain. Before I arrived I expected to encounter the most malicious, hateful, scum-of-the-earth characters. That was my image of prisoners.

During the interviews, I gained a new perspective. Yes, these men were in prison because they were convicted of a serious crime. For some their crime was a single, dumb, stupid act that they did and now deeply regret. Others had a long history of criminal activity. But their crime or crimes were not the only part of their life stories.

Some men were hooked on drugs or alcohol at an early age and had nothing resembling a normal childhood. Some never got past first or second grade. Some had physical or mental disabilities. Many grew up with little or no guidance or direction. Many had sad tales of never knowing their father. Many felt unloved and inferior to others.

The prisoners spoke of the people they love, the families they miss back home, their mother, their wife and their children. Still others spoke of their hopes and dreams, what they still wanted to accomplish when they get out of prison. Many had altruistic dreams and plans for helping others.

I was finding in these men a lot of goodness that I wasn't expecting. One day I mentioned this to the chaplain who had served in the prison for nineteen years. He smiled. Then he shared with me what his experience taught him. He said, "From my observations, I would venture that the good people in this world are about ninety percent good and ten percent bad. And the bad people? About eighty percent good and twenty percent bad." Yes, he was well aware of the sociopaths and dangerous criminals who were on death row. But his ministry brought him to see a lot of beauty deep within even the most hardened offenders.

I could find goodness inside men who were serious criminals. *What will we find with an honest look inside of ourselves?*

If we take the suggested inward journey and can't believe the good news at our journey's end, we can at least believe what the journey itself teaches. It teaches that there is no one on this planet exactly like us.

We are one of a kind.

No one has had the exact same experiences as we have had. No one has the exact same likes and dislikes, joys and fears, hopes and dreams as we do. Without each one of us, something very singular and distinctive would be missing in this world. We are irreplaceable. This sense of uniqueness is a great starting point for building a sense of self-worth.

As we observe our uniqueness along the journey within, our eyes begin to open to the uniqueness of every other individual we meet. What a gold mine of human ability and achievement there is in our family, our friends and all the people we encounter each day.

Great things happen when we start believing in our inner goodness and self-worth:

> 1. We stop comparing ourselves to others.[2] Instead we look forward to learning all we can about them and viewing them with wonder and awe.
>
> 2. The success of others does not threaten us. Instead we rejoice in their success. They have their special gifts to give, and we have ours.
>
> 3. We no longer feel the need to impress anyone. If they choose to admire us, that's fine. But we don't try to gain approval by bragging, showing off or putting others down. We don't depend on the opinion of others in order to feel good about ourselves.
>
> 4. We are free to always speak the truth. We don't fear anyone else's judgment of us because we know who we are.
>
> 5. We feel no need to gain an unfair advantage over anyone. We try to work it so that every situation is win win.
>
> 6. We don't seek confrontation, but we also don't avoid it if necessary. When a person has reached a meaningful level of respect for himself or herself, respect for others and cooperation with others follows.
>
> 7. Because we believe in ourselves, our eyes are opened to a whole new world of possibilities.

Socrates observed that the unexamined life is not worth living. We can examine our life regularly by taking the inner journey suggested in this chapter. At any level of the journey we can stop, gaze about at the bundle of life and energy we possess and grow in appreciation of the treasure that is each one of us.

We spoke earlier about the human tendency to put ourselves down. Even after we experience the forgiveness of God for our failures and sins, we may still feel inferior and think that so many others are better than we are. It is difficult to experience joy when we are feeling inadequate. Let's turn to faith for some help.

> **Who are we?** Along with our limitations and sins, we are gifted people. We have physical abilities, mental agilities, emotional and artistic capabilities, personality endowments and a wide variety of creative talents. We are alive. We can see and hear and feel. We can think and learn and reason. We can wonder and dream and imagine. We can laugh and cry, dance and sing, plan and choose. We have the breath of God, the life of God in us. We are filled with love and we can give love.

> **Who are we?** In the Book of Isaiah we are reminded that God is the potter and we are the clay. "We are all the work of your hands" (Isaiah 64:7). And, as any child of faith will point out, "God don't make junk." Despite our faults and failings, we are a work in progress. God is patiently forming and shaping us into his work of art, his "handiwork" (cf. Ephesians 2:10).

Who are we? In the book of the prophet Zephaniah, we read, "The Lord, your God is in your midst, a mighty savior; He will rejoice over you with gladness and renew you in his love, He will sing joyfully because of you, as one sings at festivals" (Zephaniah 3:17-18).

Who are we? In St. Matthew's gospel Jesus talks about our value in his Father's eyes. "Are not two sparrows sold for a small coin? Yet not one of them falls to the ground without your Father's knowledge. ... So do not be afraid; you are worth more than many sparrows" (Matthew 10:29-31).

Who are we? Whenever we are down and out, feeling worthless and unloved, we need to meditate on the death of Christ on the cross. In the Epistle of Peter, we read that we were ransomed "not with perishable things like silver or gold, but with the precious blood of Christ" (Peter 1:2). In other words, we are priceless. A price-tag of a million dollars or even a billion dollars doesn't come close to the precious blood of Christ.

We are treasure! "Where your treasure lies, there your heart will be" (Luke 12:34). In John's gospel, we have Jesus' prayer at the Last Supper. And in that prayer he states of his apostles, "Father, they are your gift to me" (John 17:24). Jesus calls his apostles—and by extension his followers today—gifts, a treasure from the Father. We can add to Luke 12:34 and say, "Where Jesus' treasure lies, there is his heart."

Imagine a large building. On the outside it is not spectacular. There is nothing unusual about the architecture. In fact, the building is rather ordinary looking, pretty much like the surrounding buildings. The walls are a bit weathered and could us a coat of paint. The roof will soon be in need of repair. Suddenly, the doors open and we get a look inside. Ah, what beauty! There is a magnificent painted ceiling, and there are elegant tapestries hanging on the walls. There are mahogany staircases, plush rugs, and elegant furnishings. There is gold and silver in the tableware, and we see diamonds everywhere. What a rich and luxurious interior!

Now imagine a group of critical people walking on the outside of the building. They don't like the building. They don't like its shape, its color, its age or its location. So they decide to tear it down. They get heavy equipment and demolish the building—without ever looking inside. What a loss of all that interior beauty. And all because the demolishers never took the time to look inside.

Look in the mirror. Chances are you see nothing extraordinary. Just an average looking person. Others too, at first glance, might not be impressed with you. Then take the time to look inside. St. Paul, in his epistle to the Corinthians, writes, "Are you not aware that you are a temple of God, and that the Spirit of God dwells in you.... The temple of God is holy, and you are that temple" (1 Corinthians 3:16, 17).

The dwelling place of God... Churches, temples, mosques and other places of worship may be decorated to the hilt with gold, silver, and diamonds. But buildings are just buildings. They have no minds and can't think. They have no wills and can't choose. They have no hearts and can't love. We are living dwelling places that think, choose, and love. The living God who is dwelling in living beings transforms our minds, wills and hearts into instruments for truth, goodness and beauty. How precious is the human person, more precious that the purest gold and more radiant than the largest diamond.

Through the prophet Isaiah, the Lord speaks these words to us. "Can a mother forget her infant, be without tenderness for the child of her womb? Even if she should forget, I will never forget you" (Isaiah, 49:15). Throughout the Bible we are constantly assured of God's love and affection. "Greater love than this no one has," Jesus said, "than to give up his life for his friends" (John 15:23). He said it. Then he did it. And he did it out of unconditional love. "While we were yet sinners Christ did for us" (Romans 5:8).

This chapter is filled with quotes from the bible to help us feel the arms of God around us. This is why we call the gospels "good news." To know that we are in the thoughts of God, crafted by God, watched over by God and loved by God brings a sense of inner joy that surpasses all understanding.

Chapter 9

Learn from Life

We are afflicted in every way, but not constrained;
perplexed, but not driven to despair; persecuted, but
not abandoned; struck down, but not destroyed.
—2 Corinthians 4:8

A reporter asked a bank president, "Sir, what is the secret of your success?"

The banker replied, "Two words."

"And, sir, what are they?"

"Right decisions."

"And how do you make the right decision?"

"One word."

"And, sir, what is it?"

"Experience."

"And how do you get experience?"

"Two words."

"And, sir, what are they?"

"Wrong decisions."

Here are some frequent occurrences: We forget to set the alarm clock and are late for school or work. We accidentally leave the glove compartment open and now our car battery is dead. We miss a last-second free throw and our team loses the game. More seriously, we give a poor presentation and lose a sale. We drink too much and say something hurtful to a friend. We run a yellow light and cause a serious accident.

When these types of experiences accumulate, it is easy to become discouraged. We start to feel inadequate, incompetent, and wonder if we are "losing it." We browbeat ourselves with self-doubt. We feel afraid to try. Sometimes we simply want to run away and hide.

How does one cope with bloopers, blunders, gaffes and faux pas? Jokingly, I state that I allow myself five mistakes a day. Yesterday I was back in bed by noon![1]

> *Strong people make as many and as ghastly mistakes as weak people. The difference is that strong people admit them, laugh at them, <u>learn from them</u>. That is how they became strong*
> —Richard Needham

Abraham Lincoln

An often cited example is Abraham Lincoln. During his lifetime he failed in two businesses, had a nervous breakdown, was rejected from law school, lost four jobs and eight elections. But he didn't quit. He admitted his failures, laughed at them and learned from them. One day he was elected president of the United States.

Colonel Sanders

Colonel Sanders thought he had a great recipe for chicken along with a brilliant idea on marketing. He tried to interest restaurant owners to go along with his product and plan, but one after another said no. In fact over a thousand restaurant owners turned him away. Finally, one decided to give the Colonel a try. Then another. Then another. And the rest is history.

Did the Colonel suffer disappointments? Yes, many times. *Was he a failure?* No, because he never quit pursuing his dream.

Dr. Seuss

Dr. Suess, a physicist whose real name was Dr. Theodor Geisel, believed he had a great approach to children's books. He submitted his work to one publisher after another.

Twenty-five said, "No." Finally, the twenty-sixth one said, "Yes!" Since them, millions and millions of children have come to enjoy his imaginative stories and illustrations. His first twenty-five attempts to get a publisher were stepping-stones to finding the right one.

Thomas Edison

Thomas Alva Edison is well known as one who "failed" 1,199 times to find the right filament for a light bulb. He kept working—experiment after experiment. Then on attempt number 1,200, he found it! In his mind, he never failed. His many unsuccessful experiments were necessary steps along the way to finding the right solution.

> *Some people say, 'You win some*
> *and you lose some.' I say,*
> *'You win some and you*
> *learn some.'*
> —Barry Johnson

Successful people give us this model for handling setbacks:

1) They know that actions are not the same as the person. They may not succeed in a particular action; e.g. they may lose an election, lose a sale, or lose a golf game. But that doesn't make them a failure as a person. They know they have talent, integrity, ideas, good will and determination. They consider themselves a success as a person, even though a particular action or project of theirs didn't work out.

2) They have a powerful dream. They are focused. They know what they are going after and they are willing to invest the energy and pay the price to get there. They don't waste time complaining about the bumps along the road because their mind is on the rainbow up ahead. And they don't let the criticism of others discourage them. It is heartening to know that, when in art school, Charles Schultz earned only a "C plus" in the course "Drawing of children." Fortunately for us *Peanuts* fans, he pursued his dream.

3) They are not afraid to try. In basketball you miss a hundred percent of the shots you don't make. In business you lose a hundred percent of the sales you don't attempt. And you certainly can't win the lottery if you don't purchase a ticket. Beverly Sills states, "You many be disappointed if you fail, but you will be doomed if you don't try."

4) They dismiss any thoughts of quitting. They believe failure is not in falling; failure is in not getting up. Obstacles merely strengthen their resolve.

When it looked like England was about to lose World War II, Winston Churchill gave speech after speech, rallying his people to continue the fight and not surrender. Some time later, after the war was won, Churchill was invited to give the commencement address at Oxford University. He is remembered as saying these words: "Never, never, never quit." Everyone knew where that speech came from. His words were an accurate reflection of how he led as Prime Minister.

> *The purpose of obstacles is*
> *to instruct, not obstruct.*
> —Mark Riesenberg

5) They learn from the experience. When something doesn't work and they fall short of their goal, successful people **learn from the experience**. When a baseball player strikes out, he may sulk and learn nothing. Or he may analyze why he went after a bad pitch, decide what he needs to work on in practice, think of how he can be better prepared for this pitcher next time and visualize himself hitting the ball.

After only 700 failed attempts to develop the light-bulb, Thomas Edison assistants were discouraged and doubted the effort. Edison told his weary workers, "Don't call it a mistake, **call it an education.** Now we know 700 things not to do!"

Jack Canfield has a brilliant way of "naming" any setbacks. He doesn't give them any losing connotation. He says that when something falls apart for us, it is the universe telling us that we are "off course." We should be grateful. Our response should be, "Thank you for telling me. I was off course. Now, let's see.... What do I have to do to get back on course on my way to success?" Each experience of being "off course" teaches us something, if we are willing to listen and not put ourselves down. Obstacles are meant to instruct, not obstruct.

> *Failure is the opportunity to begin*
> *again more intelligently.*
> —Henry Ford

Sometimes there is an easier way. Sometimes we don't have to personally experience a long series of errors in order to learn. We can observe what others did wrong, and learn from them what to avoid. Better yet, we can observe what others did to succeed and follow their example. The wheel of success has already been invented. It's okay to copy the pattern.[2]

> *This is a common theme in the folklore of*
> *Arabian Nights; where you stumble and*
> *fall, there you find the gold.*
> —Joseph Campbell

So when you feel down and out because you drove the wrong way on a one-way street, got on the wrong bus, locked your keys in the car, missed the field goal, forgot to pay a bill, arrived at a birthday party a day late, put your foot in your mouth, had to declare bankruptcy, experienced a disastrous honeymoon, or just tripped over your own two feet and fell, don't get depressed. Instead, remember:

- Your actions and you are not the same.
- Keep focused on your dream.
- Dismiss any thought of quitting.
- Keep a sense of humor.
- Ask: *What is the lesson here?*

A classic example of a person who learned his lesson is found in the story of the prodigal son in the gospel of Luke. Here was a young man who took an early inheritance, squandered it on a life of dissipation, and then found himself so down and out as to be slopping pigs for a living. With the phrase, *"Coming to his senses..."* (Luke 15:17), the gospel pinpoints his enlightenment.

He decides to return home, hoping his father will at least hire him as a worker. The father instead forgives him and reinstates him as his son. By admitting his stupidity and his sin, the son was given a chance to start over and now bring honor to his family. How would that story have ended had the son not come to his senses and learned from his mistakes?

A concluding thought:

> *If I had a formula for bypassing trouble, I would not pass it around. Trouble creates a capacity to handle it. I don't embrace trouble; that's as bad as treating it as an enemy. I do say meet it as a friend, for you'll see a lot of it and had better be on speaking terms with it.*
> —Oliver Wendell Holmes

Chapter 10

Deal with Criticism
– 12 Strategies

Blessed are you when they insult you and persecute you and utter every kind of evil against you because of me.
—Matthew 5:12

*I*magine this scene. A child wants to get up before a class to give a speech, but decides not to do it. He is afraid that others may criticize him if he makes a mistake.

A teenage girl wants to take a role in a school play, but chooses not to do it. She fears that some of the other kids will make fun of her weight.

A young man wants to run for public office, but opts out of the race at the last minute. He doesn't want his family subjected to the vicious scrutiny of the press.

Examples like these are repeated many times each day. There are multitudes of people who could have, should have or would have done great things, but decided *not to even try* because of the fear of criticism. Many of us can still remember the childhood jingle that went, "Sticks and stones can break my bones, but words will never hurt me." Not true, not true!

Karen Carpenter was a very popular singer in the 70's. Once, during an interview, someone referred to her as "chunky." Not a very flattering thing to say to a young girl. The word burrowed deep into her consciousness. She started to diet. Soon she couldn't stop dieting. She developed a serious case of Anorexia Nervosa, and eventually died of it.

What a great loss to the entertainment world. Would that the name-caller had thrown sticks and stones at Karen rather than that deadly critical word.

Chances are the first critical words directed at us occurred when we were born. I can imagine the doctor, nurse or midwife looking at you or me and saying, "This child is too light (or too dark, too fat or too skinny)." "Her legs are too short, just like her mother's." "His ears are too big, just like his father's." Right from the start somebody noticed that we were not perfect. We weren't then, and we aren't now.

So there will always be something about us that people will pick on, denounce or at least "advise" us on how we can improve. Why people do this is a complex issue, but criticize us and bully us they will. You can count on it. And this can lead to recurring depression. How do we deal with criticism?

1) Expect Critism
We should **expect criticism**. We shouldn't be surprised when it comes our way. The Philosopher Aristotle observed this twenty-three centuries ago. "Criticism is something we can avoid easily—by saying nothing, doing nothing, and being nothing."

If we are determined to speak true words, do just actions and be something worthwhile, we will ruffle feathers. Good. It means our life is having an impact. From the very first day of his public ministry to his last breath on the cross, Jesus faced harsh criticism. And he warns us, "If they persecuted me, they will also persecute you" (John 15:20). We are in good company.

2) Be Bold
We should **be bold**—not fear criticism nor run from it. Instead, we need to stand up and welcome it. If the criticism is true, we can learn from it and improve our self. This is

especially true if the criticism comes from someone who loves us and is concerned about us.

When we are growing up we need parents to teach us right from wrong by correcting us as needed. When we are in school, we need teachers to instruct us in the best ways to study and learn. When we start to work we need a boss who will point out how we can improve our performance and thereby keep our job. If we take up golf, we will need a pro to point out ways to develop our swing.

When I took a speech class in college, I always sought out a particular friend to give me feedback when I practiced my delivery. I trusted him to be honest. He not only patted me on the back when I did well, but also let me know where I messed up and where I needed to improve. I invited (key word!) his criticism. How else would I learn? To be critiqued by an audience after a real-life delivery would be too late.

3) Work in Progress
Remember that we are **works in progress**. None of us ever reaches our full potential. Helpful criticism can be the spur we need to grow and improve. The key here is not to take any criticism as absolute truth. It is only the opinion of another fallible human being. First we listen. Then *we* judge if what they say is of value. If it is, we can learn from it and grow. If it is not, we ignore it and go on.

4) We Are in Control
Know that **we are in control** of our feelings. Oftentimes criticism is spoken not to help us but meant to hurt us. Let's say a person comes up to you or me and says, "You're a stupid idiot." Our boss, our parent, our neighbor or even a stranger could speak these words. Obviously this kind of statement is meant to hurt us. *Will it work?* ONLY IF WE LET IT! Eleanor Roosevelt made this keen observation. "No one can make you feel inferior without your consent."

The key here is <u>what we say to ourselves</u> after someone says something to us. For instance, we might say, "I guess he's right. I am a stupid idiot." Then we are giving our consent to someone else's words. Or we might say instead, "Oh, the poor fellow. He must be too blind to see the goodness and intelligence I have. I hope someday he'll take the time to really know me."

We might surmise, "Wow, I wonder what's eating him. I wonder if he is sick. For his sake, I hope his attitude improves." Or again, "What a grouch. He doesn't seem to like anyone. I'll bet he would criticize Mother Theresa." In other words, we have the power to accept or reject, agree with or disagree with any put-downs, criticisms or bullying addressed to us.

5) What We Are

We must be sure of **what we are**. If someone calls me "Shorty," and I know I am six foot four inches tall, the words can't possibly hurt me. Their perception is clearly wrong. But if someone calls me "ugly," and I am unsure about how I look, the words can bother me.

If we are insecure and filled with self-doubt about our looks, our talents, or our accomplishments, then the words of others can gnaw at us. If our feelings about ourselves are anchored on a firm belief in our inner goodness and worth (cf. Chapter 7), we need not worry about words. Still, please duck from any sticks and stones.

6) What We Stand For

We must be sure of **what we stand for**. In the words of Winston Churchill, "So long as I am acting from courage and conviction I am indifferent to taunts and jeers. I think they will probably do me more good than harm." Oftentimes, the taunts and jeers of others can strengthen our resolve and spur us on to victory.

The apostle Paul was certainly one who knew what he stood for. And no opposition could deter him from his purpose. He said, "What will separate us from the love of Christ. Will anguish, or distress, or persecution, or famine, or nakedness or peril, or the sword... I am convinced that neither death, nor life, nor angels, nor principalities, nor present things, nor future things, nor powers, nor height, nor depth, nor any other creature will be able to separate us from the love of God in Christ Jesus our Lord" (Romans 8:35, 38-39).

7) Where We Are Going

We must be sure of **where we are going**. It was Leonardo da Vinci who stated, "Obstacles cannot crush me. Every obstacle yields to stern resolve. He who is fixed on a star does not change his mind." After Pentecost the apostles knew where they were going and what they were about. They kept in mind all that Jesus said and did, and what Jesus expected of them. In the Acts of the Apostles we read, "Observing the boldness of Peter and John and perceiving them to be uneducated, ordinary men, they (leaders, elders, and scribes) were amazed, and they recognized them as the companions of Jesus" (Acts 4:13).

8) Support

In the ever-bumpy journey through life, it certainly helps to have **support** from our family and friends. The early Christian martyrs facing persecution and death strengthened each other, singing and praying together right up to their last breath. Firemen have performed heroic deeds thanks to the encouragement and example of others around them. Politicians join a party to have the collaboration and backing of others who believe as they do.

Choose our friends carefully and we can count on peer support in doing the right thing. And an understanding family can be a great refuge and source of rejuvenation as we face the challenges of life. The best way to insure that our family and friends will stand by us when we need them is to be a loyal family member and a loyal friend.

9) Courage

"Last, but by no means least, courage—moral courage, the courage of one's convictions, the courage to see things through. The world is in a constant conspiracy against the brave. It's the age-old struggle—the roar of the crowd on one side and the voice of your conscience on the other." These words of Gen. Douglas MacArthur remind us that we will not always have the support of others.

There comes a time when we will have to stand alone, when family, friends, peers and colleagues, for whatever reason, choose not to support us. The dictionary defines courage as "a quality which enables one to pursue a course deemed right, through which one may incur contempt, disapproval, or opprobrium."

Once we commit ourselves to truth and justice, we have to brace ourselves for opposition. If we stand up for the right to life of the unborn, we may get voted out of office. If we stand up for the environment, we may lose our job. If we stand up for moral values in entertainment, we may get ridiculed. If we stand up for the rights of minorities, we may be rejected. If we proclaim our faith in God, we may get martyred. Our consolation comes in knowing that we are walking in the footsteps of the Master.

10) Forgive ourselves

The most harping critic we face is the one in the mirror. "I'm such a klutz." "How could I say something so stupid?" "I can't do anything right." It is imperative for our personal happiness that we squelch negativity and regularly engage in positive self-talk (cf. Chapter 2). It's okay to criticize our actions but not the person we are.

11) Give ourselves credit for trying

Theodore Roosevelt stated, "Far better it is to dare mighty things, to win glorious triumphs, even though checkered by failure, than to take rank with those poor souls who neither enjoy much nor suffer much, because they live in the gray twilight that knows not victory nor defeat."

When I was a kid, I was proud to be a fan of the Chicago Cubs, even though the team was regularly in last place. I saw the players as a bunch of guys who always gave the game their best effort. Every once in a while, when the team was behind five to nothing in the bottom of the ninth, they would amazingly pull it out and win six to five. Wow, what a team! They never gave up. When I die, I would like only two words engraved on my headstone: "I tried."

> *Criticism, like rain, should be gentle enough*
> *to nourish a man's growth without*
> *destroying his roots.*
> —Frank A. Clark

12) Ground Rule

Finally, I share with you the **ground rule** for administering criticism. Criticism, to be effective, must be accompanied by compassion and affection. This was said best by author James Dobson, in his book, *What Wives Wish Their Husbands Knew About Women.* "The right to criticize must be earned, even if the advice is constructive in nature. Before you are entitled to tinker with another person's self-esteem, you are obligated first to demonstrate your respect for him/her as a person. When a relationship of confidence has been carefully constructed, you will have earned the right to discuss a potentially threatening topic. Your motives will have been thereby clarified."

Be patient during suffering.
No winter has yet held back the power of spring.

Chapter 11

Handle Grief

And Jesus wept.
—John 11:35

I have a good friend in Chicago who is a genuine jock. We both love sports, and over the years we have played a lot of softball and basketball together. When his mother passed away, I was called upon to preside at her funeral Mass and burial. I will never forget the final service. With a large gathering of his family and friends there to pay their last respects, my friend suddenly began to cry. He progressed to wail. He carried on and on, showing his grief in no uncertain terms, hugging the casket as he moaned out loud. A lot of us were starting to get embarrassed. It didn't look cool for a strong man to be so sensitive. Finally, the burial concluded and we all left. Shortly afterwards, my friend went back to work. He felt fine.

I started to reflect... In my friend's ethnic tradition, it was very acceptable to be highly vocal and visible with grief at the burial of one's mother. He was in touch with his emotions and he expressed them. He got it all out. The next day, life went on.

Many of us men wouldn't have behaved like that. We would have been afraid to look so emotional, fearing others may think we were weak. We would have stifled our tears and not expressed our emotions so visibly. We grew up with the dictum, "Grown men don't cry." As a result we end up lamenting in silence for weeks afterward, wondering why we can't sleep, why we feel nauseous and why we can't concentrate. The lesson came to me loud and clear: All sorts of bizarre behavior results if we don't deal with our emotions at the right time and in an authentic manner.

Grief can cause long-term depression, but only if the grief is not dealt with. It is very normal to feel terrible when a loved one dies. And it is very normal to grieve and mourn for a time. If we clearly identify our grief and express it at the right time and in an authentic manner, our grief will eventually subside and life will get back to normal.

Time heals. We will always miss our loved ones. Still, the sadness of their death will not keep us from continuing on with life and functioning normally. If we don't live out our grief appropriately, time will not heal us and a dull, lingering depression will follow.

Grief occurs not only at the loss of a loved one. Grief comes whenever there is a letting go of a meaningful relationship. A marriage breaks apart, a friendship ends, a child leaves home, good neighbors move, or a fellow employee is fired. Throughout the journey of life we have to say "goodbye" many times to people who are special to us.

We spoke earlier of the "death" or "letting go" that is a passage from one stage of life to another. I remember a charming drawing that shows a young boy on a ladder, attempting to glue a colorful autumn leaf back onto a barren tree. A friend on the ground looks up and says, "Autumn is over. Let go. Let go."

It can be very difficult to let go of something we have loved and enjoyed. But there comes a time when we have to let go of our youth, our health, our abilities, our possessions and, most difficult of all, our dreams. Whenever such a "death" occurs, we need time to grieve. Otherwise a low level of sadness takes over and we wonder why we feel so down.

The soul would have no rainbow
had the eyes no tears.
—John Vance Cheney

Tears

The work of grieving involves tears. Yes, grownups do cry. Crying shows that we have advanced beyond the adolescent fear of what others may think. It shows that we are in touch with our true selves. Tears at a funeral identify us as someone who has loved another and we honestly admit we miss them. Tears are a testimony that our life with this other was meaningful, worthwhile and filed with love. Tears over any significant personal loss are the language of the soul. Tears express a depth of sorrow which is not possible to put into words.

Talk

To cope with grief it is important to **talk** about our feelings with someone who is non-judgmental and gives us all the time we need to process. The last thing we need to hear when grieving is, "Oh, you shouldn't feel that way." Or, "Come on now, get over it." A good listener will let us babble away as long as we need to until all anguish and pain is poured out, gazed upon and accepted.

It is foolish to tear one's hair in grief, as though
sorrow would be made less with baldness.
—Cicero

Rituals

Because we are physical beings with a soul, we grieve with **rituals**. At the time of death, each faith community has prayerful ceremonies to help people let go and discover reasons for hope. Besides the official funeral rites, simple rituals can facilitate our grief. Some people write a note with a personal message for the deceased and place it in the casket at a wake.

Placing flowers at the gravesite is a common expression of affection. Putting pictures of a loved one in a place of honor, lighting a candle in their memory, planting a tree in their honor, or sitting alone in the dark until dawn comes can help us through the pain.

If a love relationship ends, it helps to sing a blues song, burn love letters, wash our hands, or close a door and open another. If we are grieving over the loss of a job, it helps to make a list of the successes in our work, reflect back and feel good about the past. If we are grieving over the loss of health, holding hands with family and friends can reassure us that we are not facing the future alone.

Light griefs can speak, but deeper ones are dumb.
—Seneca

Silence
Silence is powerful. To stand at the casket and stare in silence.... To gaze upon a photo of a lost love and weep.... To sit alone by the ocean and be quiet.... Sorrows are gently washed away in stillness and solitude. In order to do its work of integration and healing, the soul needs time alone. Give it that time. The lingering distress will slowly drift away. And peace will come.

Faith
Finally, **faith**. There is an inner peace that only comes from belief in an afterlife. If we believe our God is merciful and our God "wills everyone to be saved" (1 Timothy 2:4), then the passing of a loved one in death becomes a celebration of his/her entrance into eternal life. As the poet Tagore expressed it, "Death is not extinguishing the light. It is putting out the lamp, because the full light of dawn has come."

The Lord is close to the brokenhearted.
Those who are crushed in spirit he saves.
—Psalm 34:19

When we lose a loved one, we are crushed in spirit. From the initial shock, through the denial, the anger, the sadness and then the acceptance, we have an opportunity to journey with the Lord. Jesus walked this way before us. We know he experienced the death of his foster father, Joseph. He wept at the death of his friend Lazarus. And in his ministry he must have ministered to many families who sought his help with their grief.

Jesus wants to be close to us when we are broken-hearted. He wants to assure us that through his death and resurrection he has conquered sin and death. We have nothing to fear as long as we are with him.

The death of a loved one cannot help but confront us with our own mortality. We become more aware of the fact that someday we are going to die. This awareness may be more recurrent if we are up in age, or suffering from a serious illness or going off to war. Death may not be too far away.

Even if we are young and in good health, we know that someday death will come. No one escapes it. If we are living a reasonably happy life, the thought of it coming to an end can sink us into sadness. We are sad to think about leaving loved ones, sad to recognize that our good times will cease, and sad to know that we can't take our possessions with us. Reflect on Halloween for a moment. Doesn't it seem strange, even bizarre, that some young children celebrate this day by dressing up as skeletons, ghosts, or the Grim Reaper? And isn't it odd that some people decorate their front lawn with tombstones on Halloween? Why do they do this? Isn't death something to be feared? Why do they make it an object of entertainment?

The roots for such mockery can be traced back to faith, a faith found in the first letter to the Corinthians. Here we read the words of the apostle Paul where he scoffs at death. "O death, where is your victory? O death, where is your sting?" Paul goes on to proclaim, "Thanks be to God who has given us the victory through our Lord Jesus Christ" (cf. 1 Corinthians 15: 54-57). Paul is telling us that, through faith and baptism, we are united with Christ. And because Christ died and then rose from the dead, we believe that we too will live a new life after our earthly life ends.

At a funeral Mass, we hear these words, "In Christ who rose from the dead, our hope of resurrection dawned. The sadness of death gives way to the bright promise of immortality. Lord, for your faithful people, life is changed, not ended. When the body of our earthly dwelling lies in death, we gain an everlasting dwelling place in heaven." The "goodbye" at the time of death is a temporary word. As the German proverb says, "Those who live in the Lord never see each other for the last time."

Along with the children in costumes, we too can go right ahead and mock death at Halloween or any other time of the year. Such mocking arises from a faith assuring us that death is a transition, a time of passage. This faith not only lifts us out of grief and sadness, but also helps us look forward with hope to the time of our own transformation. We are made for something eternally beautiful.

Chapter 12

Forgive & Be Forgiven

*Lord, if my brother sins against me, how often must I
forgive him? As many as seven times?" Jesus answered,
"I say to you, not seven times but seventy-seven times.*
—Matthew 18:21

*H*as anyone ever hurt you? Silly question, isn't it? When
the doctor spanked you at birth to get you breathing, it was
a fair warning that your life here on earth will have its share
of pain. At issue in this chapter is uncalled-for pain. Perhaps
as a child you were bullied by a classmate, received an
undeserved reprimand from a teacher or were treated harshly
by a coach. As an adult perhaps you have been harassed,
assaulted, robbed or raped. Maybe you have been wounded
by insults, treated with prejudice or unjustly fired. Perhaps
you are victim of political oppression, war crimes or terrorist
attacks.

Worst of all, perhaps someone close hurt you. Maybe a
parent neglected you, abandoned you or physically abused
you. Maybe a brother or sister lied to you, a spouse cheated
on you or a friend betrayed you. Maybe a sibling robbed
you of your inheritance.

If the injury or injuries were recent you may be upset
right now. If the injury or injuries were in the distant past,
you may still be carrying around some anger and hurt. Either
way, that inner pain needs to be resolved.

Resolution is accomplished by forgiveness. But
forgiveness can be difficult. You are thinking, "I am a victim
of unfair, unwarranted and undeserved treatment. How can

I forgive the perpetrator of this? How can I ever forget what he/she did?" The deeper the hurt and the more repeated the offense, the more challenging it is to forgive.

Pardon is made easier if the one who offended you offers an apology. But oftentimes they do not. Sometimes they don't even know they hurt you. Or perhaps they have passed away and are no longer able to apologize! You realize that to keep carrying the burden of anger and resentment will eventually push you down into the pits. You want to rid yourself of such a burden. But how does one arrive at a forgiving heart?

> *Could we read the secret history of our enemies*
> *we should find in each one's life, suffering and*
> *sorrow enough to disarm all hostility.*
> —William Longfellow

Know All
This quote by Longfellow echoes the Greek proverb, which states, "**Know all** and you will forgive all." If we knew the troubles and difficulties of others' lives, their abusive upbringing, their physical and emotional problems, their temptations, their addictions, their humiliations, their ignorance and/or their broken dreams, we would find much cause to be patient and understanding. Like an umpire, we can judge another's action wrong, but we cannot judge another's human heart. Only God knows what goes on inside the human conscience and how free is another's choice.

Self-Knowledge
Secondly, we have to look at our own "feet of clay." A healthy **self-knowledge** brings us to the realization that none of us is perfect. Each of us has at one time or another hurt someone. Perhaps we said something that was mean or

insulting, or did something that was insensitive and hurtful. We stood in need of another's patience and understanding. A healthy self-knowledge of our own weaknesses and limitations leads us to a forgiving heart, and moves us to go easy on others. We are disposed to both give and receive forgiveness.

When we progress through the forgiveness process, we might recall some unresolved conflicts for which we are the blame. We are the person who needs to initiate reconciliation and say "I am sorry." It is easier to say, "I forgive." To forgive is to be in charge. To say, "I'm sorry," means that we are seeking the mercy of another. This takes greater courage because there is no guarantee we will receive mercy.

> *He who cannot forgive others breaks the*
> *bridge over which he himself must cross.*
> —George Herbert

Two People Freed

Thirdly, the miracle power of forgiveness is that it sets not one but **two people free**. The one forgiven is freed from the burden of guilt and wrongdoing. And the forgiver is released from the burden of anger, resentment and bitterness. Otherwise the offender has a double power. He hurt us once. And he has imposed upon us the second burden of remembering and reliving the hurt. To forgive cancels all power of the one who offended us. By forgiving, we gift ourselves with a fresh beginning.

> *One of the secrets of a long and fruitful*
> *life is to forgive everyone everything*
> *every night before you go to bed.*
> —Ann Landers

There is a lady named Aba Gayle whose youngest daughter was brutally stabbed to death almost four decades ago. She tells the story of how she dealt with her anger and bitterness. She decided to write a letter of forgiveness to the convicted killer, who was in San Quentin prison awaiting execution. She says, "When I mailed that letter—just the physical act of mailing that letter—all the hate, all the rage, all the anger went away instantly. And in its place, it was filled with peace, love and joy." Now she gives speeches about the healing power of forgiveness. She stresses that anger and hate makes a person sick. Forgiveness makes us whole.[1]

> *The weak can never forgive.*
> *Forgiveness is the attribute of the strong.*
> —Mahatma Gandhi

A young soldier in Napoleon's army had committed a deed that was deemed worthy of death. He was sentenced to face a firing squad. The young man's mother came to Napoleon and begged for mercy for her son.

Napoleon told her, "Woman, you son does not deserve mercy."

"I know," she replied. "If he deserved it, then it would not be mercy."

"Well, then," said the Emperor, "I will have mercy."

Given enough time all people disappoint one another. We even disappoint ourselves. We browbeat ourselves because of resolutions we have not kept or ideals we have not reached. We mope about for years with regrets about something we did or said, or something we neglected to do or say. We recall our transgressions of God's laws. And like a heavy burden upon our backs, remorse and guilt weigh us down and hinder a spirit of joy. Depression sets in.

Forgive Ourselves

A forgiving heart towards others is the best guarantee of a **forgiving heart towards one's self.** Everyone, including ourselves, must be given a chance, and another, and another, as much as necessary so that useless burdens are lifted and life can move on.

> *Better by far that you should forgive and smile*
> *than that you should remember and be sad.*
> —Christina Rossetti

When we reflect on Good Friday, we picture Jesus hanging on the cross. With nails pierced into his hands, thorns pressed into his head, and welts on his back from the scourging, he was writhing in pain. Yet I doubt that the physical was the worst part of his suffering. I think what hurt Jesus more that day was looking about in his hour of need and seeing his best friends—the apostles—missing. One friend betrayed him and another denied him. The rest were off hiding some place out of fear. They outright deserted him. Only the young apostle, John, was by the cross. What a disappointment they were to him. What a failure in loyalty. What heartache for Jesus.

For the rest of Good Friday, all day Saturday and early Sunday, the apostles must have wallowed in guilt and depression. They had disappointed their Master. They sinned against the one who loved them so. They knew what armies do to deserters. How could they have been so weak!

On Easter morn Jesus rose from the dead. The apostles heard the news and doubted at first. Then they were excited... and then afraid. They were excited to learn that he came back to life. But they were afraid, wondering if he would forgive them. Would he even come to see them? They knew they had failed him. They didn't deserve to be called his friends any more. He certainly would be justified in ignoring them and recruiting new followers to do his work.

So when Jesus appeared in the upper room where the apostles were gathered, they stared at him in anxious anticipation. What would he say? Would he rebuke them? Would he denounce them? Would he call down his angels to punish them? His first words were, "Peace be with you" (John 20:19). Ah... they were pardoned! They were absolved. Now the resurrection was total Good News for the apostles! Jesus not only rose but he also forgave them. Yes, the apostles saw the wounded hands and feet of the risen Lord. They also saw the face of God, the face of forgiveness.

Shortly after, when Jesus commissioned these reconstituted apostles to go out and forgive sins in his name, they were ready. They would go forth to lavish God's mercy, because they had experienced it firsthand. They would be patient and understanding confessors, because they had received the mercy of God themselves.

Like the apostles, there were times when we have failed in our friendship with God. Perhaps we failed to worship God or failed to thank God. Perhaps we cheated somebody, were unfaithful to our spouse, did violence to another, acted unjustly, lied, or wallowed in greed, lust or pride. To break one of God's commandments is to sin. To sin is to be in need of forgiveness.

Forgiveness is not something we deserve. We cannot earn it. It is a gift from God.

So we bow down in repentance and ask, "Lord, we are sorry. Please have mercy." The message the apostles received at Easter can then be ours. "Peace be with you. Yes, I forgive you. I forgive and forget. I give you a new beginning, a fresh start on life." From the Old Testament, "Though your sins be like scarlet, they may become white as snow" (Isaiah 1:18).

Neurotic guilt gets us bogged down in self-pity. Healthy guilt moves us to acknowledge our human limitations and failings, leads us to sorrow and conversion, and helps us rejoice in the gift of loving mercy. When we are forgiven, we kick off all dejection, express our thanks and rejoice. The angel told Joseph in a dream, "You are to name him Jesus, because he will save his people from their sins" (Matthew 1:21). To trust in the mercy of God is to build our life on solid rock.

Chapter 13

Commit Yourself

I have set before you life and death,
the blessings and the curse. Choose life...
—Deuteronomy 30:19

Some time ago I took part in a discussion with a group of high school seniors. The leader of the discussion asked the question, "How do you guys evaluate your class spirit this year?" One of the participants spoke up. "I think there is too much apathy in our class." The young man sitting next to me mumbled, "So what?"

Apathy and depression are first cousins. What drives away the "So what?" attitude of apathy and generates the "Hurray!" attitude of excitement is **commitment**. Those who feel committed to a cause, a purpose, or a goal are excited to get out of bed in the morning. They are energized for hard work. They are stimulated to learn and grow. They are prepared to deal with obstacles. They inspire others to join in their parade.

People lacking in commitment wallow in cynicism, don't see much meaning in their lives, are unfocused in their thinking and disorganized in their activities. As a result they flounder about, don't accomplish much and eventually get down in the dumps and depressed.

> *We act as though comfort and luxury were*
> *the chief requirements of life, when all that*
> *we need to make us really happy is something*
> *to be enthusiastic about.*
> —Charles Kingsley

What are some symbols of commitment?

A **signature** is one. In 1776 John Hancock and the Continental Congress penned their names to *The Declaration of Independence.*

An **exchange of rings** is another symbol. By this action a husband and wife show their commitment to one another in marriage.

A **handshake**. Often a business deal ends this way. Two CEO's shake hands over their merger, promising to work together.

Passing a peace pipe. Native Indians did this to show their commitment to a peace treaty.

Raising our right hand or placing it over our heart when we make the "Pledge of Allegiance" symbolizes our commitment. We show our intent "to support and defend the Constitution and laws of the United States of America.... (and) bear true faith and allegiance to the same" (From the Oath of Citizenship).

Let's reflect for a moment about *The Declaration of Independence.* What if our Nation's founders said, "I think independence is a good idea. I'm all for it...as long as it doesn't take too much time...as long as I don't lose any money...as long as I won't get hurt." Fortunately, they didn't place any conditions or reservations on what they were about to do. They were *totally* committed. They proclaimed, "We mutually pledge to each other our lives, our fortunes, and our sacred honor." They signed their names boldly in ink, not pencil. There were no wimps among them.

How about marriage? What if a husband or wife said, "Yes, I'm in favor of this marriage. I think I'll give it a try and see how it works." Pretty weak commitment, right? A plastic ring would be a good symbol of that kind of attitude. Instead we hear couples publicly proclaim their love, "for better, for worse, for richer, for poorer, in sickness and in health, until death do us part." Their engagement ring is set with a diamond, the symbol of strength and endurance. Their wedding rings are made of gold forged in fire. By wearing these rings a husband and wife are reminded of their unbreakable bond to one another.[1]

Whether the important issues in our life are political, relational, social, financial or personal, to arrive at a solid and long-lasting commitment is not easy. We will need to study and reflect, discuss and analyze, consider various alternatives, seek advice and turn to prayer.

Once we decide to commit, amazing things happen. Our whole being gets involved. The doors of our imagination and creativity open up. Our inner resources are tapped. We discover a quality of energy unknown to the wishy-washy.

Commitment rallies our courage, stiffens our backbone and toughens us for all challenges. Commitment opens our senses and our intuition, alerting us to new opportunities that the universe is suddenly providing.

> *Until one is committed, there is hesitancy, the chance to draw back, always ineffectiveness. Concerning all acts of creation, there is only one truth: That the moment one definitely commits oneself, then Providence moves, too.*
> —Johann Wolfgang von Goethe

Commitment clarifies who we are. We hammer out our identity by naming our values and choosing our goals. When we stand for something, it means we won't fall for everything. We have set our feet on solid ground.

Commitment excites others and brings them aboard. Commitment draws the world around us into our dream, enlisting help from others.

Every time a man stands up for an ideal, or acts to improve the lot of others, or strikes out against injustice, he sends forth a tiny ripple of hope. In crossing each other from a million different centers of energy and daring, those ripples build a current that could sweep down the mightiest walls of oppression and resistance.
—Robert Kennedy

People on fire with commitment have no time for self-pity. "Oh, poor me. Nothing is going right. Nobody cares." They don't waste precious time with that. They have things to do, places to go, people to greet and challenges to meet.

People driven by commitment are not procrastinators. In fact, they often get a jump on their work in hopes of achieving their goal sooner.

People stimulated by commitment don't sweat the small stuff. They have their sights fixed on a star and can't be bothered with the little bumps along the way.

Hearts governed by commitment experience a joy that goes beyond accomplishment. Even if they fall short of reaching the immediate goal that they are striving for, they find an inner peace knowing they gave their best effort.

Do you want to compete in the Olympics, climb Mt. Everest, run for president, own your own company, have a successful marriage, enjoy a happy family, lose weight or improve your golf game? The question is, "How much do you want it?" How much thought and preparation are you willing to give to it? How much time and energy will you expend on it? How much are you willing to sacrifice for it?

It has been wisely noted that little people have wishes, while **great people have a purpose**. Great people pursue that purpose with their chins firmly facing the wind, their eyes never looking back. Committed people are stickers and fighters, not escape artists. They renew their vows or commitments often, even daily. They do this out loud. They keep focused at all times.

It is important to commit to a purpose that is worthy of us. Otherwise we may reach our goal and then suddenly realize that we wasted our time and energy. It would be like the man who reached the top of the ladder of success only to find out it was leaning against the wrong wall.

It is in choosing a purpose that a person of faith turns to God. What is his will for us? What are the genuine needs of our human family? What are the talents we have been given to respond to these needs? How can we make a difference for good in our world?

*There has never been a statue erected to the
memory of someone who let well enough alone.*
—Jules Ellinger

*The hottest place in hell is reserved for those
who in the time of great moral crisis
maintain their neutrality.*
—Dante

At first glance, the suffering and pain of our human family seem overwhelming. What can we possibly do to make a difference? Where do we start? Should we even dare to begin? Who will help us? I find hope in these words from Clarissa Pinkola Estes:

> *I have heard from so many recently who are deeply
> and properly bewildered. They are concerned about
> the state of affairs in our world right now. Ours is a
> time of almost daily astonishment and often righteous
> rage over the latest degradations of what matters most
> to civilized, visionary people.*

You are right in your assessments. The luster and hubris some have aspired to while endorsing acts so heinous against children, elders, everyday people, the poor, the unguarded, the helpless, is breathtaking.

Yet, I urge you, ask you, gentle you, to please not spend your spirit dry by bewailing these difficult times. Especially do not lose hope. Most particularly because, the fact is that we were made for these times. Yes. For years, we have been learning, practicing, been in training for and just waiting to meet on this exact plain of engagement.[2]

Whether we dedicate ourselves to teaching or healing, whether we join the Peace Corps or Mothers Against Drunk Driving, whether we use our talents and energy to fight poverty and hunger, work to protect human life, reach out to the homeless or battle against global warming, we will succeed if we work "with all our heart, all our soul and all our mind." No winter can hold back the spring determined to blossom. No darkness can extinguish the light we have received from the Light of the World.

Total commitment is what Jesus asks of his followers. He tells us to love the Lord God "with all your heart, with all your soul and with all your mind" (Matthew 22:37). We are to let nothing and no one get in our way. "No one who sets a hand to the plow and looks to what was left behind is fit for the kingdom of God" (Luke 9:61).

Jesus was totally committed to doing his Father's will, even to the point of death on the cross. He says, "Do this (offer ourselves to the Father) in memory of me" (1 Corinthians 11:24). Through our remembering and sharing in the Eucharist, Jesus' strength is now our strength. We can commit without counting the cost. Easter joy is sure to follow.

Chapter 14

Use Your Head

After three days they found him (Jesus) in the temple, sitting in the midst of the teachers, listening to them and asking them questions, and all who heard him were astounded at his understanding and his answers.
—Luke 2:46-47

*I*magine that you are walking along the seashore, enjoying the fresh air, the soft sand, and the sound of the waves. Suddenly you see something ahead of you that sparkles like nothing you've ever seen before. You go to pick it up and discover that you just picked up a diamond. Wow!

Then you notice another diamond at your feet. You pick that one up. Then you see another, and another and another. So you hitch up your pants, roll up your sleeves and set out to pick up as many diamonds as you possibly can carry. You go about dancing and singing for you know you are becoming very rich.

A fantasy? Not at all. Right now, today, you and I have the opportunity to pick up an endless supply of diamonds. These diamonds no one can take away from us. We can give them away and still not lose them. I am speaking about the diamond-like riches of knowledge.

A day in the life of the learned is worth more than the whole life of the ignorant.
—Seneca

Our brain thirsts for knowledge. It enjoys information to process, concepts to wrestle with and ideas to refine. That's what it is made to do. We may breathe a sigh of relief when our days of formal schooling are over, i.e., no more homework, papers, exams, etc. But the moment we wake each morning, school is back in session. Ongoing education opportunities are presented to us every day. If our brain doesn't show up, expect trouble.

An inactive brain results in the painful demerit of a stagnant life. We become less aware and less competent. Judgments are made in ignorance. Emotional responses are unbalanced. Conversation dwindles into petty gossip and quips about the weather. As we notice people around us who read and grow in intelligence, we start to feel stupid. Eventually we become anxious, lose confidence and get depressed.

> *Life is tough. And it's even*
> *tougher if you're stupid.*
> —John Wayne

Did you hear about the young man who went to college on an athletic scholarship, but failed to apply himself to class work? A teacher observed, "He is going to flunk. The handwriting is on the wall. Unfortunately, he can't read."

What are some of the payoffs of education? A better job? Very likely. We've all read statistics that show how a higher level of education translates into a higher income. But education is concerned with more than making a "living." It's about making a "life."

For starters, learning dispels boredom. Our brains are able to process information faster than our senses can supply data. We need not worry about "tired brain syndrome." It doesn't exist. Our body may get tired and our senses need a break. But the brain, like a powerful battery, keeps on going. Benjamin Franklin was once asked, "What kind of man deserves the most pity?" He answered, "A lonesome man who does not know how to read." Boredom and depression are kissing cousins.

High Adventure

Learning propels us into **high adventure**. Our minds can travel into the spheres of science and mathematics, the realms of art and literature, the domains of philosophy and history, and unlimited vistas of opinion and truth. Our minds find great joy in searching and seeing, thinking and understanding, questioning and resolving, and giving in to wonder. We acquire a sense of power as we name reality. We experience a feeling of humility as we gain insight into the mysteries of being and existence. Life expands to cosmic dimensions.

> *The growth of the human mind is still high adventure, in many ways the highest adventure on earth.*
> —Norman Cousins

Self-Discovery

Learning leads to **self-discovery.** As we are introduced to ideas, facts, people and things, we find ourselves in relationship to them. We learn the boundaries of our present self and the possibilities of our future self.

Perhaps some who are reading this are thinking, "That's all very nice. But I can't afford any more education. Colleges and universities are too expensive." Going to a reputable college and listening to learned professors is certainly desirable. But often it is not possible.

My father only had four years of formal education. He completed eight grades in four years. Then at age twelve, being the oldest of six children, he went off to work to help support the family. But my father had acquired a love of learning. And for the rest of his life he read everything he could get his hands on, constantly beating a path to the public library. He became a writer and was one of the most intelligent persons I have ever known. He, like many successful people, became quite learned and did so with limited formal education.

A trivia question: *Which of the following never went to law school?*

- John Jay, first Chief Justice of the Supreme Court
- John Marshall, Chief Justice of the Supreme Court
- William Wirt, Attorney General
- Daniel Webster, Secretary of State
- Samuel Chase, Chief Justice of the Supreme Court
- Abraham Lincoln, President
- Stephen Douglas, Senator, Representative
- Clarence Darrow, Defense Attorney in the Scopes Trial in 1925.
- Robert Storey, President of the American Bar Association
- Strom Thurmond, Senator, Governor of South Carolina

Clarence Darrow was the only one of the above who went to law school, but only for a year. He preferred to study on his own. Whatever schooling the other men experienced in the beginning of their lives got them "off and running" to use their brains and study throughout life.

Here is a sure-fire way to judge the quality of any academic institution:

If a student graduates and says, "Boy, I'm glad that's over—now I can go out and get a job...."

School rating: <u>F-</u>

If the student graduates and says, "Wow, what a great introduction to learning. What great habits I've acquired. I can't wait to see what else I can learn during the rest of my life."

School rating: <u>A+</u>

The object of education is to prepare the young to educate themselves throughout their lives.
—Educator, Robert Hutchins

We live in a country where the opportunities for lifelong learning abound. Besides schools, libraries and museums, there are learning channels on TV, instructional DVD's, books on tapes and CD's, and access to encyclopedic knowledge by way of the Internet. And nothing can replace the mental stimulation that comes from conversing with intelligent people, especially if they are in your family.

Josiah Henson was an orator, an ex-slave who became a leader in the early abolitionist movement. One day he was introduced to the archbishop of Canterbury. The archbishop, impressed with Henson's bearing and speech, asked the name of the university at which he studied. "The university of adversity" was Henson's reply.

Although he was a Son, he learned obedience through what he suffered.
—Hebrews 5:8

Knowledge, Understanding, and Wisdom

If we combine formal education with personal study and with reflection on experience (the university of adversity), our minds will leap from ignorance to **knowledge, understanding,** and **wisdom.**

That was how the apostles learned. "Learn of me," Jesus told them, "for I am meek and humble of heart" (Matthew 11:29). The apostles did not attend theology classes. They grew in knowledge about who Jesus was by walking with him day after day, watching him work, eating with him and conversing with him. Slowly the apostles came to realize that they were in the presence of the Son of God. By example Jesus taught them how to pray, how to preach and how to wash the feet of one another. He taught them how not to fear. He showed them how to live and he showed them how to die.

The apostles were challenged to learn a lot in a brief time. They needed extra help to put it all together. So at Pentecost the Holy Spirit came upon them and gifted them. They came to understand the meaning of all Jesus said and did. And they were given the wisdom and courage to live out that meaning. Their intellectual life and moral life were intertwined and led them down the path to eternal joy.

> *This is eternal life, that they should know*
> *you, the only true God, and the one*
> *whom you sent, Jesus Christ.*
> —John 17:3

We began this chapter talking about diamonds. Jesus is the pearl of great price (cf. Matthew 13:46). May all our learning lead us to him.

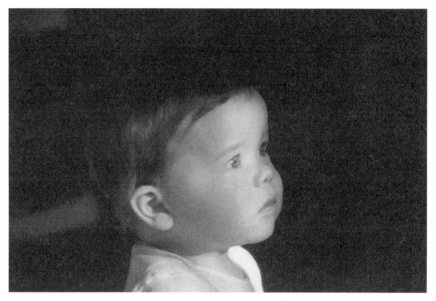

To see the world with the eyes of a child means never to be bored.

Chapter 15

Nourish Your Soul

Whatever is true, whatever is honorable, whatever is just, whatever is pure, whatever is lovely, whatever is gracious, if there is any excellence and if there is anything worthy of praise, think about these things.
—Philippians 4:8-9

*A*s our minds long for truth, our souls long for beauty. The beauty of a sunset, the beauty of rose, the beauty of a sonnet, a beauty of a symphony, the beauty of a Sistine chapel, the beauty of a newborn child.... Without beauty, life would be one drab thing after another. Everyone would be despondent.

To cope with ordinary bouts of gloom, we need to seek out beauty, surround ourselves with beauty, and provide the time for beauty to fill up our senses and flood our soul. The experience of the beautiful resonates with the deepest recesses of our being, enabling us to understand the unity of all creation. The experience of the beautiful escorts us into wholeness and joy.

Climb the mountains and get their good tidings. Nature's peace will flow into you as sunshine flows into trees. The winds will blow their freshness into you, and the storms their energy, while cares will drop off like falling leaves.
—John Muir

Our starting point for our journey into beauty is nature, the "great outdoors." John Muir lived in California—and for good reason. This state has eight hundred miles of ocean shoreline, range upon range of foothills and mountains, abundant flora and fauna, along with redwood forests and desert wasteland.

Some time ago I was standing in line at a local Auto Club. To kill time I picked up a book off a nearby rack and began thumbing through it. *Scenic Drives in the USA* was the title. The book listed forty-eight scenic drives in California, so I tried to note which ones I still needed to explore. Then, out of curiosity, I checked on the number of scenic drives in other states. One state (I won't reveal its identity, but it's in the Midwest) had only one scenic drive listed. A couple of other states had three. Like John Muir, I am grateful to be living in a state where nature struts some of her finest stuff.

The gloom of the world is but a shadow. Behind it, yet within reach, is joy. There is radiance and glory in the darkness, could we but see. And to see, we have only to look. I beseech you to look.
—Fra Giovanni (1513 A.D.)

If you live in that state with no mountains, no ocean, and only one scenic drive, are you out of luck as far as nature is concerned? I don't think so. Just step outside at night and survey the sky. How many of the ten thousand visible stars can you count? (You may have to get away from city lights for this.) Observe a firefly, catch a snowflake, scrutinize a leaf, walk barefoot through the grass, smell new cut hay, feel the bark of a tree, pet a dog, ripple with the wind—and even *listen* to the field corn. (Some claim it can be heard growing!)

If we open all our senses, we'll be amazed how much beauty surrounds us, no matter what state or where in the world we live. Then, once our senses are fine-tuned to find beauty in nature, our soul is primed to search for beauty in every conceivable human experience.

> *We form our architecture. After that*
> *our architecture forms us.*
> —Winston Churchill

Drab architecture depresses the soul. Exciting architecture lifts up the soul. Since architecture has such power to form us, how about the all the other components of our physical surroundings? One very effective tool for combating depression is to fashion and shape our daily environment so that it is saturated with beauty. When a colorful, positive, and pleasing atmosphere surrounds us, our gloom is dispelled and our spirits rejoice.

Let's examine our surroundings. Is there quality art hanging on the walls where we live, work, study and play? How about sculpture? Is there a garden nearby? Do we have Beethoven's music stimulating our ears? Are the clothes (and jewelry?) we wear expressive of joy and hope? Is our everyday living space clean and orderly? Is our furniture in harmony? Do we have plants and flowers gracing each room? Is our dining table attractive? Is our home blessed with a dog, cat or canary?

If all the physical "stuff" that surrounds us affects our mood, why not make all the elements of our environment as beautiful and as positive as possible? A gray and tired environment feeds a gray and depressed soul. An artistic and pleasing environment gives off positive vibrations that stimulate the soul.

If of thy mortal goods thou art bereft, and from
thy slender store two loves alone are left, sell one,
and with thy dole, buy hyacinths to feed thy soul.
—Saadi, 12th Century Persian Poet

Thoughts are an essential part of our inner environment. So we need to "decorate our minds" with attractive, elegant and noble ideas and insights (cf. Chapter 2). Is there good literature within arm's reach of our favorite chair? Do we play recordings of poetry while we drive? Do we watch TV programs that invigorate our mind? Do we seek out conversation with intelligent, creative and imaginative people? Do we avoid people who are grumpy and hypercritical?

How do we spend our leisure time away from home? Do we budget for concerts? Do we frequent museums, botanical gardens and the zoo? How often do we stroll through a park? Do we choose to watch movies that spark noble emotions?

It is personal participation that burrows us into a soulful life. That means we not only need to listen to good music, but we need to sing, dance, and/or take up a musical instrument. We should not only read good literature, but we should take up a pen (or word processor) to write poetry, prose or a diary. We must not only stroll through a garden, but we ought to plant flowers, groom trees and grow vegetables. Involvement is key.

The sky is the daily bread of the eyes.
—Emerson

Emerson was right. But we do not live on bread alone. For our soul to be fulfilled, we need to provide a feast of beauty for all of our senses. We must to be constantly on the lookout for new ways that beauty can pervade all the times and places of our lives. The effort to meet this challenge will be exciting and will itself prod us out of depression!

Productive work, love and thought are possible only if a person can be, when necessary, quiet and alone with themselves.
—Erich Fromm

For a soulful life, three things are necessary: group time, pair time and alone time. The most challenging is to be alone with oneself, far from the sound of other people's voices, and far from the noise of other's people's agendas. This time alone opens for us a wide gate leading into wisdom and peace.

The soul of a person immersed in work and in serving others longs for the beauty of solitude. It is necessary. In solitude the soul catches its breath. In solitude the soul lets experiences seep in. In solitude the soul sifts out what it wants to remember and throws the rest away. In solitude the soul cultivates a sense of wonder, awe and appreciation. In solitude the soul comes to know itself. In solitude the soul finds God.

A talkative barber was trimming the beard of King Archelaus, and asked, "How shall I cut?" The king answered, "In silence,"

In Mark's gospel we read, "Rising very early before dawn, he (Jesus) left and went off to a deserted place, where he prayed" (Mark 1:35). To balance the frenetic pace of his preaching and healing ministry, Jesus needed a time and a place to "catch his breath." In the desert Jesus found the solitude that enabled him rest and be alone with his Father.

In the desert Jesus must have spent a lot of time contemplating his Father's creation. So much of his preaching included allusions to the birds of the air (Matthew 6:26), to the flowers of the field (Luke 12:27), to seeds growing (Matthew 13:4), to the fig tree (Luke 13:6), to sheep (Luke 15:1), to the mountains (Luke 23:30), and to the vine and branches (John

15:1). The soul of Jesus was in communion with the world of nature that his Father crafted so lovingly.

Depressed people often run away from solitude. They are afraid to be alone. But once the lesson of chapter seven (self-esteem) is fully integrated, these same people long for solitude. They like themselves and find joy in being alone with themselves. After spending a period of time strolling the inner landscape of their souls, they are able to return to the hustle and bustle of everyday life. They feel more integrated and more self assured.

> *Hurry, scurry*
> *Worry, flurry*
> *There go the grownups*
> *To the office, to the store*
> *Subway rush, traffic crush*
> *No wonder grownups don't grow anymore*
> *It takes a lot of slow to grow.*
> —Eve Merriam

If we surround our lives with the beauty of nature, art, literature and music, and if we bask in the sunshine of solitude, we are equipped to radiate beauty and goodness to others. We can awaken their souls to the richness that life has to offer. We can arise out of our sometime-dispirited state of being and bring a fresh vitality to others.

Most importantly, if we contemplate and immerse ourselves in the gorgeousness that surrounds us, we transcend it.

> *For from the greatness and the beauty of*
> *created things, their original author,*
> *by analogy, is seen.*
> —Wisdom 13:5

Chapter 16

Ah!
The Turning Point!

Unless the grain of wheat falls to the ground
and dies, it remains just a grain of wheat;
but if it dies, it produces much fruit.
—John 12:24

As I mentioned earlier, when I was still in postgraduate studies, I had an opportunity to work at the Illinois State Prison in Statesville, IL. This was a large maximum-security institution, with over three thousand prisoners. High walls surrounded the complex, with guards everywhere. Each morning, as the chaplain's assistant, I entered the prison through five gates. Then these gates were locked behind me. The walls of the prison were so high that no one inside could see outside. There were no menus. Everybody ate the same food out of the kitchen. When a prisoner needed to go from one building to another, he would sign out when he left and sign in again when he arrived.

When evening came, I would walk through those five gates and go back into the outside world. Meanwhile, the prisoners remained behind the walls, locked into their cells for the night. I began to sense what a blessing it was to be free, to be able to move about and act as I chose.

I know a lot of people who are in prison. However, the prison that holds them is not a state penitentiary. It is a prison of their *own* making. They are all walled in on themselves. They can't see beyond their own needs into the world of other people. Chains of selfishness and self-centeredness hold them down.

Maturity is a long journey—
a journey out of oneself.
—Anonymous

The only way out of the "prison syndrome" described above is to say, in effect, "Hey, I have a lot of problems. I'll bet there are others out there who have problems, too. I *wonder* if I can help them. I *suspect* I can. In fact, I *know* I can. I *choose* to help them." This is the **TURNING POINT!**

Now the focus shifts. We think, plan, and work for the well-being of others—not just for our self. In the process, we often forget about our self. We break free from the "me-first" attitude. Egocentric walls tumble down. The chains of pleasure-seeking melt off. We gain the liberty to grow and be our best self in the interest of our fellow human beings

There are two types of people—those who
come into a room and say, 'Well, here I am!'
and those who come into a room and say,
'Ah, there you are.'
—Frederic L. Collins

If you ask an engaged couple why they want to get married, they may answer, "Well, I want to settle down." "I want to have a home of my own." "I want to be happy." All very normal answers—for starters.

Hopefully they will eventually say, "I think I can make her happy." "I want to provide her a home." "I want to care for her health." "I want to give him a hand to hold, a shoulder to lean on." "I want to give him support and encouragement." In other words, when the focus is off the self and onto the other—their happiness, their well being, their needs being met—then the couple is ready for marriage. Marriage guarantees nobody happiness. It guarantees a lifetime of opportunity to bring happiness to another.

There is a story told about the comedian, Jimmy Durante. During World War II he was asked to take part in a show for some veterans. He agreed but said he was on a tight schedule and would only have time to do one of his short monologues. However, once he got through his short monologue, he stayed on stage and continued performing. The applause grew louder and louder and he continued on for thirty minutes. Finally, he took a bow and left.

Backstage someone asked him, "I thought you had to go in a few minutes. What happened?" "I did have to go," Jimmy responded, "but I can show you the reason I stayed. Look in the front row." There in the front row were two veterans, each of whom had lost an arm in combat. One has lost his left arm, the other his right. They were enjoying the show so much that they hit their two remaining hands together in order to clap. And clap they did. Durante felt inspired to give them the best he could.

The famous psychiatrist, Dr. Karl Menninger, was once asked what a person should do if they felt a nervous breakdown coming on. His reply, "Lock up your house, go across the railway tracks, find someone in need and do something to help that person."[1]

A good example is Dr. Patch Adams. As a young man he was institutionalized with suicidal depression. While in the institution he discovered he had a talent for making people laugh. He went through medical school, got his degree, and now incorporates joy and laughter into his healing practice. If you are looking for ideas on how to reach out and help someone and have fun in the process, see: www.patchadams.org.

A human being is happiest and most
successful when dedicated to a cause outside
of his own individual selfish satisfaction.
—Dr. Benjamin Spock, Pediatrician

Jesus told us that he came that we may "have life and have it more abundantly" (John 10:10). Then he showed us how to have this life. At the Last Supper he got down on his knees and washed the feet of his disciples. Afterwards he told them, and us, "If I, therefore, the master and teacher, have washed your feet, you ought to wash one another's feet" (John 13:14). It is in service to our brothers and sisters where we find purpose, meaning and fulfillment of life on earth.

If we find that the walls of selfishness and self-concern imprison us, it means that it is time for us to turn around, refocus and discover the joy of giving. This requires a profound "death to self," putting aside our personal concerns. It involves turning our inner spotlight onto the happiness of those around us. Seeking the good of others is the turnkey that effectively unshackles us from feelings of depression.

> *What makes loneliness an anguish is not that*
> *I have no one to share my burden, but this:*
> *I have only my own burden to bear.*
> —Dag Hammarskjöld

The first miracle of Jesus recorded in the gospels was the miracle at Cana. Jesus turned water into wine. We can take our cue from that and realize that our vocation is to go through life turning water into wine. We are called to turn...

> ...the water of tears into the wine of laughter.
> ...the water of sadness into the wine of hope.
> ...the water of loneliness into the wine of friendship.
> ...the water of inequality into the wine of justice.
> ...the water of indifference into the wine of compassion.
> ...the water of conflict into the wine of peace.

It is God's grace that liberates us for this work. We are now free to spread joy.

Chapter 17

Go to Work

*We instructed you that if anyone was unwilling
to work, neither should that one eat.*
—2 Thessalonians, 3:10

Remember the seven dwarfs? With smiles on their faces and a bounce in their step, they marched around singing: , *"Hi-Ho! Hi-Ho! It's off to work we go."* Is that you? If not, why not? There are many fortunate individuals who begin their workweek with a tank full of gusto. Their occupation is challenging and the atmosphere of the workplace is amiable. They look forward to enjoyment and pleasure in their jobs.

For many others Monday morning is a drag. You can see them driving the freeways or waiting to board the bus with a look of pain on their faces. If they had the energy to sing, their song would resound, "Oh, Woe! Oh, Woe! It's off to work we go." Yes, a lot of depression today can be identified as simply the **work-place blues.**

A lot of what passes for depression these days in nothing more than a body saying that it needs work.
—Geoffrey Norman

Wrong Job

So why is work sometimes such a drag, a drain and the cause of dejection? Some people are depressed because they know they are in the **wrong job** and therefore their talents and abilities are not being used effectively. They find their jobs dull, monotonous and without meaning. These are the clock-watchers who, at the end of the week, utter the popular phrase, "Thank God it's Friday." They may not be deeply depressed, but for forty hours a week their happiness quotient is close to zero.

Inadequate Recognition
There are others who do not receive **adequate recognition** or receive a less than adequate salary.

Too Much Work
There are those who have over-demanding jobs, whose problem is **too much work.** They have to put in so many extra hours of time and energy that they have become stressed out, burned out. They long for retirement.

Tough Relationship
The problem for some is a **tough relationship** on the job. They are working with someone or for someone that they cannot get along with.

Unemployment
Worse off are those who are **out of work**. They have been fired or let go. They search the want ads, can't find a job and their bills keep piling up. This situation creates high anxiety and intensifies depression.

Lazy
Finally, there are those who are **lazy**. They work as little as possible and can't figure out why they feel down.

Did you hear about the three men who were worked in a quarry? The first was asked, "What are you doing?" Without expression he replied, "I'm working hard to earn a living."

A second man was asked the same question, "What are you doing? He barked back, "Can't you see I'm constructing a wall?"

The third man was asked the question, "What are you doing?" With a smile on his face and a lilt in his voice he enthusiastically responded, "I'm helping to build a cathedral!"

It's a matter of **perspective.** If you are a bank teller, are you making a living, counting money or helping people put order into their finances? If you are a bus driver, are you earning a paycheck, driving a vehicle or helping to transport people safely to their destination? If you are a carpenter, are you working your shift, hammering nails or providing a home for a family?

> *Work is love made visible.*
> —Kahlil Gibran

It is important to distinguish our *job* from our *work*. Our job is what we get paid for doing. Our work is what we do to make life better for our fellow human beings. If we see our jobs as just doing a task, we will want to get it over with. But if we see ourselves as serving other human beings, there's a good chance we will be enthusiastic and want to give our work the best effort we can.

Maybe we are in the right job but have the wrong attitude. For instance, the job we get paid for is checking out groceries at a supermarket. That's respectable. But our "work" involves being cheerful when we greet shoppers, encouraging others on the staff, offering help or advice and, when possible, a smile, a joke, a kind word and a listening ear. Rest assured that this kind of work takes greater effort and is more challenging than any job could ever be.

If God simply handed us everything we want,
He'd be taking from us our greatest prize—
the joy of accomplishment.
—Frank A. Clark

Unproductive Job

Some people have low-grade depression because they feel they are in an **unproductive job.** These people shuffle papers and go to meetings, but by the end of the day can't measure any accomplishments. For these people I recommend productive work at home that can be measured. If we wash the car, cut the grass, do the laundry or paint a wall, we can look back and see that we have done something worthwhile. Even better, if we wash the car of an elderly neighbor or cut the grass for someone who is ill, we will feel proud of what we have done. Each day we like to feel that we have accomplished something. Cooking a meal will do this for some. Reading a good book can give a sense of achievement, too.

Happiness is the full use of your
powers along lines of excellence.
—John F. Kennedy

Not Appreciated

Maybe we get depressed because we work to the point of excellence, but are **not appreciated** and don't receive a salary based on our worth. Housewives fall into this category. They don't get paid for what amounts to a twenty-four hour a day job, seven days a week. Women who don't receive the same wage as men for doing equal work are also in this category.

Also in the category are people with college degrees forced by necessity to take a job that doesn't utilize their education.

If for any reason we feel our work contribution is not appreciated, than we know how *millions* of other people feel. Maybe our "work" at this stage of our life is to lavish appreciation on others struggling in under-acknowledged jobs. I guarantee that our "pay" will come in an overwhelming feeling of satisfaction.

> *The happiest people seem to be those who are producing something; the bored people are those who are consuming much and producing nothing.*
> —William Ralph Inge

Job Stress

There is no easy answer to **job stress**. But a beginning approach is to ask ourselves some questions. Is the pressure upon us because we chose an extremely demanding career, i.e., brain surgery? Is the pressure there because our boss is overbearing and wants to squeeze every ounce of production out of us? Is the pressure there because we want to earn more to keep up with the Jones? Are we running away from the demands of marriage and family by putting in extra hours on the job?

Have we failed to develop other interests and all we know how to do is work? Is the stress caused by the difficulty in getting along with a boss or co-worker? Does the stress spring from a lack of balance in our lives? The experience of stress and burnout can be a wake-up call to examine and perhaps rearrange some priorities in our life, and then take action.

Too Lazy to Work

Some people suffer from self-inflicted sadness that comes from being **too lazy to work.** Do you know anybody who fits this category? Yes, there are chronic couch potatoes. They may be adult children still living off their parents when they could be out working. These adult children plan to get around to making a living someday, but not right now. They have it too good. There are the ESPN addicts who are living off their wife's salary, but plan to find a real job after the World Series is over—or maybe after the Super Bowl.

Couch potatoes get despondent very easily. Many come to hate themselves when they recognize they have been irresponsible and have not been productive. Depression that results from laziness is a well-deserved "reward." Those who choose inactivity when work is available choose the feelings that result from it.[1]

> *There is joy in work. There is no happiness*
> *except in the realization that we have*
> *accomplished something.*
> —Henry Ford

Work is essential to the fulfillment of the human spirit. So how do we get rid of the work-place blues and starting singing, *Hi-Ho! Hi-Ho?*

> 1. We will find fulfillment when our talents and skills are being put to good use, when we are earning a decent living and when we are contributing to the betterment of our world.

> 2. We will find peace when we are in the right job and performing it to the point of excellence, with opportunities for creativity and responsibility.

> 3. We will find contentment in our work when our environment is safe and attractive.

4. We will find satisfaction when our work time is balanced with family time and fun time.

5. We will find enjoyment in our work when we receive adequate pay, recognition and appreciation.

If all these pieces are not in place yet, I suggest we look for ways to make others happy on their job. That will keep us busy enough to get our minds off our temporary anguish.

> *Indeed, we hold that by offering his labor to God a man becomes associated with the redemptive work itself of Jesus Christ, who conferred an eminent dignity on labor when at Nazareth He worked with His own hands.*
> —Vatican II, *The Church Today*

Work has been labeled "Adam's curse." Throughout much of human history, work was viewed as something necessary but to be avoided whenever possible. In contrast, St. Benedict saw work in a much more positive light. His Holy Rule, based on the gospels, emphasized work and prayer as the two steps necessary for holiness of life. We need to remember that story about the three men working in a quarry. Each of the men was doing the same work, but one realized he was building a Cathedral. *All* good and decent labor can be "Cathedral Labor" if, as the statement from Vatican II affirms, we offer that labor to God.

> *Love your work. Love the people with whom you work. From love and goodness will spring also your joy and your satisfaction.*
> —Pope John Paul II

Chapter 18

Laugh

There is... a time to weep,
and a time to laugh.
—Ecclesiastes 3:4

*P*icture this: You are a doctor and a patient comes to you complaining about depression. You diagnose that this depression is not pathological, just a bad case of the blahs and blues. What would you advise?

Well, there are drugs that you could prescribe, drugs that are supposed to lift up a mood. But when the drug wears off, the person may get depressed again. Besides, all drugs have side effects and these side effects can be bothersome.

Three Laughs Every Hour
What you want to prescribe is something that is natural, long lasting, with only good "side effects." So you prescribe a medicine that will alter the person's attitude and approach to life. You sit down with your note pad and write: **Three laughs every hour**.

Now, if your patient isn't very creative, he or she may need some help with this prescription. So, as the doctor, you proceed to make a list of things the person could do to get him or herself to laugh.

What would you put on that list? Off the top of my head, here is what I would suggest:

1. Read the comics in the daily newspaper.

2. Go to a bookstore and browse through the joke books.

3. Go to a card store and read through the humorous cards.

4. Rent a comedy movie.

5. Go to the public library and borrow recordings of old time comic radio shows.

6. Go to the circus and watch the clowns.

7. Go to the zoo and notice how the monkeys look at you.

8. Get a group together and play charades.

9. Throw a Halloween party during the cloudy days of February or March—with prizes for the best costume.

10. Go to the grocery store and read the headlines of the tabloids.

11. Read your high school yearbook where you and your classmates stated your plans for the future.

If possible, do all of the above with someone who has a highly contagious laugh.[1]

Laughter is a form of internal jogging.
—Norman Cousins

Make Someone Else Laugh

A second and more potent prescription may be needed. This Rx is very effective: Go out and **make someone else laugh.** It has been wisely observed by George Gordon Lord Byron that, "All who joy would win must share it. Happiness was born a twin." Nothing gets your minds off your own problems quicker than focusing on the needs of others. When you see someone else who is down in the mouth, take it as a challenge to get him or her to laugh. Even a slight grin counts as a victory. Perhaps you could volunteer to be a clown at a children's hospital or nursing home.[2]

Smile

A third suggestion to cure depression is simply to force your mouth to **smile.** Try it. Even if you have to force it at first, you'll find that the mere outward physical act of smiling will quickly affect your inner emotions. For encouragement, sing a few bars of the song, *Smile,* by Charlie Chaplin. A big grin on your face will quickly spread to others. At the very least, it will make them wonder what you are up to.

Laugh at Yourself

Finally, learn to **laugh at yourself**. When I was a kid I used to help my dad with some of the repair jobs around our house. At times I would hit my thumb with a hammer, spill a can of paint, or trip over the lawn mower. My father would say to me, "You must be twins. One kid couldn't be so stupid." He said this with affection, hoping it would help me to laugh at myself. It worked. I learned not to take myself too seriously. If slapstick is funny on the movie screen, it is funny in real life. It has never been difficult for me to speckle my days with physical and verbal bloopers.

My four-fold prescription for depression:

1. Choose activities that cause you to laugh.
2. Make others laugh.
3. Put a smile on your face.
4. Laugh at yourself.[3]

Only those who are capable of silliness can
be called truly intelligent.
—Christopher Isherwood

In September 1862, President Lincoln called for a meeting with his closest advisors. When they arrived they found him reading a book. It was titled, *A High-Handed Outrage at Utica*, by Artemus Ward. At one point Lincoln laughed heartily but no one joined in. The advisors sat in stony disapproval of the President's frivolity. Lincoln remarked, "Why don't you laugh? With the fearful strain that is upon me night and day, if I did not laugh I would die, and you need this medicine as much as I do."[4] Then, turning to business, he proceeded to inform them about a draft he had prepared called the *Emancipation Proclamation.*

Besides being good medicine for stress and depression, another effect of laughter is physical healing. William Fry, professor emeritus at Stanford University, is a pioneer in laughter research. He says that laughter increases blood flow and contracts abdominal muscles, and that a hearty belly laugh can give us the equivalent of ten minutes on a rowing machine.

A good laugh relaxes muscles, alleviates tension and massages our inner organs. Laughter accompanied by tears and sweat releases toxins from our bodies. One study made in 1997 showed that laughter even helps prevent heart attacks. Twenty-four heart attack patients watched comedic shows for thirty minutes a day. Twenty-four other heart attack patients served as a control group. After a year, many patients in the second group had suffered repeat heart attacks compared to only two in the first group. According to Lee Beck of the University of California, Irvine, who helped run the study, laughter decreases levels of two key stress hormones that cause irregular heart rhythms which may lead to heart attacks.

> *I've seen what a good laugh can do.*
> *It can transform tears into hope.*
> —Bob Hope

There are roughly sixty-five hundred languages spoken around the world. This can create quite a communication problem. But the one language all of us humans understand is laughter. We can instantly interpret, "ho-ho," "ha-ha," and "he-he." Whether it's a little giggle, a mild chuckle or a huge guffaw, laughter communicates a shared experience of enjoyment. Laughter can help us appreciate one another as brothers and sisters and lead us to feel like one family once again. Laughter can help alleviate the worldwide depression that comes when nations fear one another.

> *Every day is miserable for the depressed, but*
> *a lighthearted man has a continual feast.*
> —Proverbs 15:15

The gospels don't record that Jesus laughed. But in chapter eleven of St. Matthew's gospel Jesus repeats what his enemies were saying about him. "The Son of Man came eating and drinking and they said, 'Look, he is a glutton and a drunkard'" (Matthew 11:19). Jesus' enemies were able to make this accusation because they often saw him attending parties.

We know he was at a wedding feast in Cana. He dined with Matthew, Zacchaeus, Martha and Mary, Peter's family and probably many others. Weddings and dinners are occasions of fun and laughter. When he fed the five thousand it must have created a picnic atmosphere. And I suspect his friend Peter was good for a few laughs now and then.

Laughter is the shortest
distance between people.
—Victor Borge

It was very important to Jesus that his followers be united. He prayed "that they may all be one, as you, Father, are in me and I in you" (John 17:21). To be one means to be free of fear and prejudice, free of anger and unforgiveness, and free of false pride and jealousy. What helps demolish such barriers is humor.

When people laugh they do not perceive each other as young and old, rich and poor, educated or uneducated. It matters not what country each person comes from or what is the color of their skin. They are simply a group of human beings enjoying a slice of life together. I believe that Jesus, knowing how important humor is for a strong community (as well as for mental and physical health), must have frequently encouraged laughter among his followers.

I feel sure he was pleased when centuries later his follower, St. Teresa of Avila, prayed, "From sour-faced saints, deliver us, O Lord."

Why choose to crawl when you have all the potential to soar?

Chapter 19

Have a Dream

Then afterward I will pour out my spirit upon all mankind. Your sons and daughters shall prophesy, your old men shall dream dreams, your young men shall see visions.
—Joel 3:1

A policeman spots a young orphan walking the streets of a big city. What amazes the policeman is seeing the smile on the young boy's face.

"Son, do you have a home?"

"No sir... not yet."

"Do you have any money?"

"No sir...not yet."

"Do you have any friends?"

"No sir...not yet."

"Then why are you smiling?

"I have a dream, sir, I have a dream."

Happy are those who dream dreams and are ready to pay the price to make them come true.
—Cardinal Leo Suenens

Few things cause depression as much as lack of direction. We wander about not knowing where we are going or why we are here. Living without meaning, we mope and brood, pine and pout. The cure is simple: choose a worthwhile dream.

Just as food and drink are essential for the life of the body, dreams are essential for the life of the soul. On the cloudiest, dreariest day, you can spot a big smile on the face of someone starting out on a vacation, someone buying a new home, someone about to graduate, someone with an engagement ring in his hand, someone off to make a sale or someone concluding a peace negotiation. With a dream in our head and hope in our heart, we are alive. Energy overflows. Goodwill abounds. There is joy.

What makes human beings different from all other species upon this earth is the capacity to dream. Our minds are capable of envisioning all types of worlds. Our imaginations can picture new places to go, fascinating people to meet and a better society in which to live. We dream of peace. We dream of love. We dream of riches. We dream of.... The possibilities are endless.

> *Great minds have great purposes, others have*
> *wishes. Little minds are tamed and subdued*
> *by misfortune; but great minds rise above them.*
> —Washington Irving

Do you want to know someone well? Ask what it is that he or she dreams about and hopes for. Our conscious dreams reveal much about our character. If our dreams are centered on improving the lot of humanity, it shows that we have a noble heart. If our dreams are only about our personal gain, we still have a lot of growing up to do.

Ask a young person who is engaged why they want to get married. They might say, "Because I want to be happy." Good luck. The chances of being disappointed are endless. No one can live up to another's self-centered expectations. But if the engaged person says, "I want to spend my life making my husband/wife happy," that's a workable dream. The opportunities of bringing joy to another are endless.

When the focus of our attention is on the *other* person, their happiness, their health, their wholeness and their well-being, there is love. A dream centered on the growth and fulfillment of one's spouse will lead to a successful marriage.

What makes dreams come true?

Well-Prepared

Dreams come true when we are **well-prepared**. If we dream of touring exotic places, we prepare by saving our money. If we dream of becoming a world famous doctor, we prepare by going to medical school. If we dream of becoming a renowned pianist, we practice, practice, practice. The "will to succeed" has to include the "will to prepare." No one can excel in a football game on Sunday if he doesn't stay physically fit, study the game plan and go to practice all week long.

> *Commitment unlocks the doors of imagination, allows vision, and gives us the 'right stuff' to turn our dreams into reality.*
> —James Womack

Dreams come true when they are powered by **total commitment**. We need to choose dreams that elicit our whole-hearted dedication. Commitment unlocks the doors of imagination and creativity, taps our inner resources and unleashes a quality of energy unknown to the wishy-washy. Commitment rallies our courage and toughens us for disappointments. Commitment draws the world around us into our dream, enlisting help from others and alerting us to opportunities that the universe is suddenly providing. Commitment draws us to prayer and opens our hearts to divine guidance.

Nothing happens unless first a dream.
—Carl Sandburg

Visualize Results

Dreams come true when the results we want are clearly and constantly **visualized**. We need an unmistakable picture of the end we are striving for. We have to fix our imagination on what it is we want to accomplish and how we will feel when it is realized. It is important to be specific. Vague dreams will produce vague results. We will not know how to prepare. Specific dreams give us important goals to strive for, and pinpoint the steps we need to take.

If our dream is to graduate from college, we begin by circling the target date on your calendar. Then we visualize our self walking up to get our diploma, the sun shining, the crowd cheering and our parents jumping for joy! The happy feelings that result from such a picture in our mind will energize us for the challenges ahead.

Whatever you can do, or dream you can do,
begin it. Boldness has genius, power and
imagination in it. Begin now.
—Johann Wolfgang von Goethe

Courage to Begin

Dreams come true for people who have the **courage to begin.** A successful dream has many gears to power us. But first we must turn the key and start the motor. Gazing out the window and simply imagining our self in some beautiful place far away can be a relaxing reverie, but it will get us nowhere. We have to put aside all doubts and fears, place one foot in front of the other and commence in the direction we want to go. The momentum will come and the excitement will build. But first we have to dare to take that first step.

*Dream no small dreams. They have no
power to move people's hearts.*
—Daniel Burnham

Stick-to-a-tiveness

Dreams come true for people who have **stick-to-a-tiveness**. In the 1920's George Mallory and his friends tried to scale Mt. Everest. Their first expedition failed, as did their second. In their third attempt, an avalanche hit and Mallory and many in his party were killed. Sometime later the survivors held a banquet to honor the memory of Mallory and his brave companions. At that banquet one of the survivors spoke, addressing a huge picture of the mountain. He said, "Mount Everest, you defeated us once, you defeated us twice, you defeated us three times. But Mount Everest, we shall someday defeat you because you can't get any bigger and we can!" In 1953 Sir Edmund Hillary reached the top of that mountain.

*What is America about? America is about the
uncrossed desert, the unclimbed tree. It is the
star that is not reached, and the harvest that is
sleeping in the unplowed ground.*
—Lyndon Johnson

Worthy Dreamers

Finally, dreams come true to those who are as **worthy and high-minded as their dream**. Mahatma Gandhi dreamt of an India independent of foreign control. Martin Luther King, Jr., dreamt of an America with equal rights for all. Walt Disney dreamt of an amusement park that would make millions of children happy. Respectively, these dreams were born out of loving hearts committed to justice, equality, and the happiness of others.

Jesus set before us a dream that is most worthy of the human heart. We claim this dream and pray for this dream when our voices ring out, "Thy kingdom come. Thy will be done." We envision a world of patience and forgiveness, and a world of justice and peace. We long for the day when all human life is reverenced, respected and cherished from the moment of conception on to natural death.

We imagine life on this earth where all the hungry are fed, the sick are cared for and all refugees and homeless people are sheltered. We picture the day when the very planet our Creator gave us is nurtured and protected so intelligently that future generations will be guaranteed clean air to breathe and fresh water to drink.

> *Without a vision the people perish.*
> —Proverbs 29:18

Can this dream become a reality? Only if we visualize it clearly, desire it completely, commit ourselves enthusiastically, take steps to it daily, pray earnestly and never give up. It is the dream that calls forth the very best that is in us. It challenges us to work together as one family under God for the good of all. The effort we put forth for this dream assures us that we are on the road to wholeness, holiness and joy.

> *For I know the plans I have for you, declares the Lord, plans to prosper you and not harm you, plans to give you hope and a future.*
> —Jeremiah 29:11

Chapter 20

What About Money?

For where your treasure is,
there will your heart be also.
—Luke 12:34

_H_as this ever happened to you? You are watching a basketball game on TV. The score is tied. Your team has the ball. There are ten seconds left to play. You are on the edge of your seat and...there is a break for a commercial! #@%!&!

It's not only upsetting that commercials come at the most inconvenient time. It's also upsetting because what they communicate to us is a lie. I don't mean that they are lying to us about a specific product. This may happen. It's the **big lie** I'm talking about. Commercials tell us over and over again, "To be happy, you've got to have this stuff. To be happy you've got to have beer, cars, perfume, clothes, medicine, cereal, etc."

It is estimated that by the time a child enters first grade, he or she has seen over 30,000 TV commercials. Thirty thousand times they have heard the message, "To be happy, you've got to have stuff."

After hearing the message so many times, some people are actually dumb enough to believe it. So they go off and buy lots of stuff. This stuff doesn't seem to make them happy. So they work harder, get more money and go off and buy more stuff. Still no happiness. So they work even harder, get more money and buy even more stuff. Still no happiness. Guess what? It doesn't work. They are looking for happiness in all the wrong places.

I remember attending a lecture some years ago on the topic of capitalism. The speaker noted that many Europeans refer to American capitalism as "savage capitalism." Savage capitalism comes from our inability to speak the words, "Enough. We don't need any more." Not being able to say "enough" leads to brutal competition, overwork and disregard for the common good. In a word: greed.

So many Americans never ask the question, "What's the economy for?" Rather than working to live, they live to work. Is it any wonder that stress, burnout, high blood pressure and depression are among our serious health problems?

I saw the opposite attitude a few years ago when I was visiting a foreign country (which will remain anonymous). I went to a shopping area around four in the afternoon and noticed that many of the stores were closed. I asked someone at the hotel where I was staying if this day was a holiday or if there was a strike going on. He replied, "No. The shop owners probably made enough money for the day, closed up and went home." In other words, the shop owners said, "Enough."

A lot of stores in this country closed early on Saturday and hardly any stores were open on Sunday. (Ah, remember those days?) Instead of seeing people working, I saw families having fun together. I saw old men on benches playing chess. I saw couples leisurely strolling hand in hand. I saw people sitting in restaurants conversing, listening to music and dining leisurely. The pace was certainly different than what I was used to. It had a spirit of calm and balance, not frenzy and greed.

Know When to Say *Enough*

I suggest we take some advice from (of all places!) a commercial. One popular commercial gives this advice:

Know when to say, *Enough!* The product of this commercial is beer, but we can apply those words to all material things. Does a rich man own a fortune, or does the fortune own him? To say, "Enough" assures us ownership of our soul, and a feeling of inner freedom. We set limits. We are in control.

Prioritize

A second step is to **prioritize.** Making a living is important. But nobody on their deathbed moans, "Gee, I wish I had spent more time at the office." When people look back on their lives, they often regret not spending more time with family and friends, not spending more time at their hobbies, not spending more time reading or enjoying nature, and not spending more time nourishing their souls. Imagine that we had only six months to live. How would we use our time and energy for these last six months?

Notice Who Is Happy

A third step is to look around and **notice who is genuinely happy.** I find it is the people who have compassion for the poor, people with a spirit of hospitality, people who reach out to those who mourn, people who forgive, people who have courage in the midst of trials, people who work for peace and people who share their possessions. In other words, living the "Beatitudes" (cf. Matthew 5:1-12) leads to being a blessed and happy person.

If you watch CNN news, you are familiar with the reporter, Anderson Cooper. He is the son of Gloria Vanderbilt. Because his mother was rich and famous, many rich and famous people visited their home when Anderson was a child. In a recent interview he stated:

> To me, the greatest privilege of the way I grew up was realizing at a very young age that these people are just as unhappy as everyone else. Once you realize

that, it frees you up from believing that fame or riches are going to bring you happiness. I think it takes a lot of people a long time to figure that one out.

For some, it never happens. The actor Jim Carrey put it this way. "I wish everybody fame and fortune so they can cross it off the list and move on to something else."

The poor man is not he who is without a cent, but he who is without a dream.
—Harry Kemp

Maybe we are richer that we thought. Among the many gifts God gives us is the ability and freedom to dream. And if our dreams include the good of others, as it does when we pray "Thy kingdom come," then riches beyond our imagination will come our way. For God rewards the generous heart. An English proverb states it this way, "The hand that gives, gathers."

One of my favorite Broadway musicals is *Annie.* The play centers on the early life of a poor orphan. She has no toys and hardly any clothes. Her prize possession is her non-pedigree mutt named Sandy. As the story evolves, a very rich man named Oliver Warbucks takes Annie into his home. Oliver Warbucks has everything money can buy—an elegant mansion, servants, fancy clothes and abundant food. Nevertheless, something is drastically wrong in his life. He doesn't know what. When Annie enters his life, he begins to realize what was missing.

At one point of the play, one of the characters in the play proclaims that, with Annie in this home, every day is Christmas. Annie is rich in things that money can't buy—personality, charm, wit, enthusiasm, a sense of wonder and love. She is the true millionaire, not Oliver Warbucks. All he can give people are things. Annie can give happiness. As the play progresses, Annie transforms Oliver Warbucks into a truly rich man, that is, a warm human being.

Instead of sitting in our counting house counting all our money, it is wise to take an inventory of the riches we have that money can't buy. In the process of spending these spiritual assets, we become even richer. There is the fortune we share when we give of our time, our talents, and our energy. There is wealth that is bestowed by our kindness and patience. There is the gold we give when we lavish forgiveness. What gems we provide when we offer a listening ear and an understanding heart. How much we enrich others when we give the gift of total attention.

And most importantly, we have been given a great fortune that is our faith. Every day we have opportunities to share this faith by both our words and example, thereby leading others to Christ, the treasure beyond price.

Once there was a tourist passing through an ancient village. In this village lived a wise old man whom the tourist had read about. So he thought he would stop by and visit him. When he entered the wise man's house, the tourist noticed that there was hardly anything in it, just a chair, a bed, some food—the basics.

The tourist asked, "Where are your clothes, books, TV, and belongings?"

The wise man answered the tourist, "Where are yours?"

"Mine?" The tourist thought. "I don't have any right now. I'm just passing through."

The wise old man paused, smiled, and said, "So am I—so am I."

If a person gets his attitude towards money straight, it will help straighten out almost every other area in his life.
—Billy Graham

Once we get our personal value system in order, there is a further task. There is the larger world scene. You and I may not cheat or steal in the local market place, but there is something else that needs to be done. Love and justice requires that we keep working and praying for peace and for the end to wars and violence.

Former General and President Dwight Eisenhower once said, "Every gun that is made, every warship launched, every rocket fired, signifies in the final sense a theft from those who hunger and are not fed, those who are cold and are not clothed." He is saying that not only do thieves rob banks, but there is grand theft when tax dollars are misdirected and misspent. Wars destroy lives and end dreams. As a result, all of us are impoverished.

What a pearl of great price we would have if the vision of the prophet Isaiah should come to pass. "They shall beat their swords into plowshare and their spears into pruning hooks; one nation shall not raise the sword against another, nor shall they train for war again" (Isaiah 2:4).

Chapter 21

Be Grateful

I thank you, Lord, with all my heart.
—Psalm 138:1

A young man approached an elderly guru and asked him to share the secret of a happy life. The guru responded, "Pay attention."

"Okay," said the young man, "I'm paying attention. Now tell me your answer. What's the secret of a happy life?"

"Pay attention," the guru repeated.

"Hey, I'm hanging on to your every word." The young man said. "Speak."

Once more the guru stated, "Pay attention."

These were the only words the guru spoke, over and over again. Eventually the young man caught on. The guru's advice for happiness was simply to pay attention to all that is in us and around us.

This is the basic message of this chapter. Oftentimes all that is needed to lift oneself out of the doldrums is to wake up, take note and **pay attention** to life's gifts and blessings. As the sign at the railroad crossing alerts us, "Stop. Look. Listen." If we do that often enough, our moodiness will drift away and we will discover what one writer discovered:

God is always coming to you in the Sacrament of the Present Moment. Meet and receive Him there with gratitude in that sacrament
—Evelyn Underhill

Some years ago, I met a young lady who was confined to a wheelchair. She asked me, "Father, what will heaven be like?" Before I could respond, she answered her own question. "You know what I want to do in heaven?" With great emotion she continued, "I want to run! I want to run... and run... and run!"

I thought to myself, *I can go outside this very moment and run. No big deal. But for this young lady confined to a wheelchair, running was most certainly a big deal, something she longed for with all her heart.*

To be able to run would have brought great happiness to her. It was her image of heaven. Her passionate longing to run helped me "pay attention" to the delights of everyday life which I had so often taken for granted. Running has since become one of those ordinary activities for which I am very grateful.

In 1977 I was planning a trip out West to visit my brother. Since I expected to see some beautiful scenery, I decided this would be the right time to invest in a quality camera. I purchased such a camera and proceeded to take it out for a test run through downtown Chicago. When my inaugural roll of film came back from the developing lab, I knew I was hooked. I discovered a "third eye." I began to see things I never noticed before: colors, textures, faces, flowers, architecture, and sunsets. These things were always around me, but now I was seeing them in a new way.

I began focusing in on details, observing angles and dimensions, discerning nuances of color and watching for balance. I started clicking away at panoramic vistas, close-up views, still shots and action scenes. Composing a picture became a delightful challenge. Each roll of film brought new excitement, an excitement that continues to this day with my digital camera. Photography has helped me to "pay attention" to my existence, expanding my awareness and increasing my amazement. I am so deeply grateful.

*One way to open your eyes is to ask yourself,
'What if I had never seen this before? What if
I knew I would never see it again?'*
—Rachel Carson

A group of children were studying the many ancient and modern wonders of the world. At the end of the course they were asked to list what they personally thought were the Seven Wonders of the World. The following got the most votes:

1. Egypt's Great Pyramids.
2. Taj Mahal.
3. Golden Gate Bridge.
4. Panama Canal.
5. Empire State Building.
6. St. Peter's Basilica.
7. China's Great Wall.

However, there was a quiet little girl who hadn't turned in her paper yet. The teacher asked if she was having trouble coming up with seven. The girl replied. "Yes, I am. I can't quite make up my mind because there are so many. The teacher suggested, "Tell me what you have so far and maybe I can help." The girl picked up her paper and read, "I think the Seven Wonders of the World are:

1. To touch.
2. To taste.
3. To see.
4. To hear.
5. To run.
6. To laugh.
7. To love.

The little girl was very astute. She was aware that there are many impressive "wonders" that we humans have built. But she also knew that *we* couldn't build anything, if it were not for the wonders of who we are and all that we can do. We can see and hear and feel. We can think and learn and reason. We can wonder and dream and imagine. We can laugh and cry, dance and sing, plan and choose. We can give and receive love. We have mental abilities, physical agilities, emotional and artistic capabilities, personality endowments and an array of talents yet undiscovered.

If we "pay attention" to all we've been endowed with as human persons, we are well on the road to awe and gratitude, enough to lift us out of our sometime depression.

> *People go abroad to wonder at the heights of the mountains, at the huge waves of the sea, at the long courses of the rivers, at the vast compass of the ocean, at the circular motions of the stars; and they pass by themselves without wondering.*
> —St. Augustine

My father died when I was 16. And one of the lingering regrets of my life is that I never adequately thanked him for all he did for me. I'm sure I gave him a card each year on Father's Day, but I could have done a lot better than that. I was just too self-centered as a kid to be aware of what my parents had done and were doing for me. I took them for granted. *Now* is always the right time to **say thanks**—to our parents, our grandparents, our children, our friends and neighbors, our teachers and our clergy, our policemen and firemen, our doctors and dentist, to any and all who have helped us any way.

It is not enough just to "pay attention" to life's blessings. We have to express our gratitude—to God, and to other people. In thanking others, we lift up their spirits. And in lifting up their spirits, we feel better about ourselves, too.

> *When thou hast truly thanked the Lord for*
> *every blessing sent, but little time will then*
> *remain for murmur or lament.*
> —Hannah More

There was a medical doctor who wisely used psychology in his practice. For patients who came to him with symptoms of stress, worry, discouragement and fear, he prescribed that they express appreciation to everyone who did them a good turn. The doctor was aware that the very act of saying "thank you" required a smile to get it right. As expected, many of his patients admitted to him that they really did feel better. And it didn't raise their insurance premiums.[1]

In the gospel of Luke we read about ten lepers who approached Jesus and asked to be cured. Jesus told them to go and show themselves to the priests. And on their way the lepers were cleansed. However, only one returned to thank Jesus. We can imagine the look of disappointment on Jesus' face when he asked, "Where are the other nine? Has none but this foreigner returned to give thanks to God" (Luke 17:17-18)?

> *Gratitude unlocks the fullness of life. It turns what*
> *we have into enough, and more. It turns denial*
> *into acceptance, chaos to order, confusion to*
> *clarity. It can turn a meal into a feast, a house*
> *into a home, a stranger into a friend. Gratitude*
> *makes sense of our past, brings peace for today*
> *and creates a vision for tomorrow.*
> —Melody Beattie

The apostle Paul advises us to make gratitude a way of life. "Be thankful... Whatever you do, in word or in deed, do it in the name of the Lord Jesus, giving thanks to God the Father through him" (Galatians 3:15, 17).

Every Catholic is familiar with the prayer, *Grace Before Meals*. "Bless us, O Lord, and these thy gifts which we are about to receive from thy bounty through Christ our Lord. Amen." I suggest we say this prayer not only before each meal, but also before every important event of the day, e.g. before going off to school or off to work, before going to a movie or on a trip, before sitting down to a concert or meeting a friend, before entering a garden or watching a sunset, etc. This will help us "pay attention" to everything that is a gift. And we will live each day in a constant state of gratitude.

This prayer can also be said before we go to bed at night. Each breath and each heartbeat during the night is a gift from our loving God. "Bless us, O Lord..." With this prayer on our lips, I suspect we will fall asleep with a big smile on our face.

Chapter 22

Be a Friend

A faithful friend is a sturdy shelter; he who finds one finds a treasure. A faithful friend is beyond price, no sum can balance his worth.
—Sirach 6: 14-15

Friendship is not difficult to identify. We all know when it is present.

Something clicks. Another person enters our life and we feel like they have always been there. They instinctively understand us, genuinely like us and share many common interests with us. We don't feel any need to impress them, nor they us. We are simply comfortable together, sharing laughter and tears, secrets and fears. And we trust that they will be there for us, today, tomorrow and always.

Yes, friendships happen. And they are beautiful. However, not all of them last throughout our lifetime. For instance, we have school pals, people with whom we share a lot in common for four years, eight years, or however long we are in a particular school. But after graduation, we move to different places, get jobs, marry, and rarely get together again.

The same kind of friendships develops among people in the Army, and in our place of work, and with neighbors, members of the PTA, coaches, etc. We are friends for a while but, as life goes on, we move away, interests change, and these friends are gradually reduced to Christmas card contacts.

These friendships are meaningful for a time but eventually they fade away. And that's fine. Not all friends are meant to be forever. It's okay to say "yes" to temporary friends. They make up a large portion of our lives.

Hold a true friend with both your hands.
—Nigerian Proverb

And then there are the deep and lasting friendships. They are few and they are rare. The friendships that last do so because the individuals have worked at it. They make sure that they are always there for each other, not just in the good times but in time of need as well. Friendships will always be tested. And it is by sacrifices and scars that friendships are proven.

While Lord Byron and Robert Peel were school mates at Harrow, a senior boy began to beat upon Peel unmercifully. Since Byron had a clubfoot, he saw nothing to be gained by his joining in the fight. Nevertheless Byron approached the bully and bravely asked how many stripes he was intending to inflict upon his poor friend. "What's that to you?" the bully thundered. And Bryon bravely replied, "Because, if you please, I would take half."

Affirmation

Friendships that last have certain characteristics. First, there is **affirmation**, that is, unconditional regard. It seems trite to say it but a friend is someone who likes us. They believe the best about us and are not judgmental about our intentions. They cheer us on and want us to succeed. In fact our success is their success, so closely do they identify with us.

Understanding

The second characteristic is **understanding.** When someone takes the time to listen to us, to tune in to us, eventually they understand what it is like to be us. This is especially helpful when trouble comes. In times of difficulty, most people don't want advice, nor do they want sympathy. They just want to know that someone understands what they are going through (cf. Chapter 5 on Listening).

Knowing that someone else understands makes our burdens lighter. We are able to face the day, because we feel we are not facing it alone. Someone knows what's happening deep inside of us. They make the time and take the effort to sense our inner world, and they treat it with respect and reverence as one treats precious china.

> *Trouble is a sieve through which we sift our*
> *acquaintances. Those too big to pass*
> *through are our friends.*
> —Arlene Francis

Grace

The third characteristic is very similar. A friend is someone who **puts up with us.** That sounds simple, but it isn't. It may be more difficult than giving up one's life, because it means giving someone another chance, again, and again, and again, as much time and space as they need. We all hate it when we stumble and fall. We may flunk a test, drop the ball, mess up a sale, lose a job, get drunk or neglect our responsibilities. At times we say dumb things, act rashly and sin. Sometimes we even hurt those who love us the most. We feel like kicking ourselves all over the block.

It is a truly mature and loving friend who, when they see us make a fool of ourselves, knows we haven't done a permanent job. So they wait. What a freeing feeling it is to know that we have someone who patiently puts up with us in our weakness, is there to help us laugh off our doubts and fears, believes we are worth knowing and wants to be with us, no matter what. A true friend helps us forgive ourselves. A true friend is a rock.

> *The world is so empty if one thinks only of mountains, rivers and cities. But to know someone who thinks and feels with us, and who, though distant is close to us in spirit, this makes the earth for us an inhabited garden*
> —Goethe

We can't demand that someone become our friend. We can't force friendship. Friendship just happens when two people "click." The best way to prepare for friendship is by being the best person we can be. When we are unselfish, generous and kind, people will be attracted to us. When we are open, truthful and keep our promises, people will grow to trust us. And when we remove the focus off of ourselves and show genuine interest in others, they will want to hang around with us.

> *Each friend represents a world in us, a world possibly not born until they arrive, and it is only by this meeting that a new world is born.*
> —Anais Nin

At the Last Supper Jesus talks about friendship. First he alerts his apostles that they will soon recognize how deep his love is for them.

"No one has greater love than this, to lay down one's life for one's friends" (John 15:13). Then he tells them how they can always be his friends. "You are my friends if you do what I command you" (John 15:14). Finally, he reminds them that what he taught them is a sacred trust from his

Father. "I no longer call you slaves, for a slave does not know what his master is about. I call you friends, because I have told you everything I have heard from my Father" (John 15:14).[1]

After walking with Jesus for three years the apostles were slowly learning that sacrifice, loyalty and truth are what bind a community to God and to one another. Jesus taught them this, "so that my joy may be in you and your joy may be complete" (John 13:11).

> *Liking people is one of the most important ingredients for getting the most out of life. If you like peopole, you have a zest, an enthusiasm for working and for living—you give of yourself to others and, in return, you find yourself getting a great deal from them. Once it becomes part of you, it will pay dividends not only in your work but in the sheer enjoyment of living. Try it, and see for yourself!*
> —Samuel Goldwyn

Nobody can go back and start a new beginning,
but anyone can start today and make a new ending.
—Maria Robinson

Chapter 23

Take Control

Blessed are the single-hearted,
for they shall see God.
—Matthew 5:8

Sometimes we find ourselves depressed because our lives are "out of control." We are always running late, eating or drinking too much, not sleeping well, saying the wrong thing, losing things, wasting time, taking on too many commitments, accomplishing little and not achieving our dreams.

We say lament ourselves: *If only I were more organized. If only I had more time. If only I could lose weight. I wish I hadn't done that. I regret that I said that.* Our lives are falling apart because we simply lack discipline.

We must all suffer one of two things: the pain
of discipline or the pain of regret or
disappointment.
—Jim Rohn

Discipline

To lead a disciplined life, the first step is to take full responsibility for our lives. I remember a story about a child asking his grandfather if he had served in World War II. The grandfather replied, "No, I didn't because of my feet." "Your feet?" inquired the child. "Yes," said grandpa, "my feet were in Canada." Feet are very obedient. They have no will of their own. They do whatever we tell them.

I know a man who blamed his weight problem on his wife's good cooking. The wife defended herself saying, "I don't put the fork to your mouth." Hands are very obedient, too. They do whatever we tell them.

Discipline is a matter knowing we have full control of our feet, our hands, indeed all our actions as well as all our dwelling thoughts. That means we take full responsibility for our lives and don't blame anyone or any outside force for our choices and our behavior. We are at the controls.

> *He who reigns within himself and rules his*
> *passions, desires, and fears is more than a king.*
> —John Milton

Goals

The next step in discipline is to decide what our life's goals are and then prioritize the use of our time in view of these goals. In a hospital emergency room, there is a triage nurse. His or her job is to examine each patient in the waiting room and decide how important their illness or injury is. The most serious cases get immediate attention. The others have to wait their turn.

In life we have to triage our time. Each day we have twenty-four hours for our use. If we know what our life's goals are, we easily decide how to use these twenty-four hours for what is truly important. If we are not clear in our goals, we will often just fritter away our time, run in all directions, and accomplish little of importance by the end of the day.

> *I have spent my days stringing and*
> *unstringing my instrument while the song*
> *I came to sing remains unsung.*
> —Rabindranath Tagore

Objectives
After we set our **goals**, we need to settle on **objectives**, that is, things we want to accomplish in the immediate future.

Plan
Next we write out a **plan** for each day and for each week.

Evaluate
After that we have to take time to **evaluate** how we did at the end of each day and each week. What did we accomplish and where did we waste time and effort?

Reward
The final but very important step is to **reward** ourselves if we have been successful. Take in a movie, go to the beach, go out dancing, etc.

For instance, I may choose as a **goal** to lose unneeded weight. My **objective** may be to lose five pounds a month. My **plan** will include listing what foods I will eat, what foods I will avoid and what exercises I will do. Every two weeks I will get on the scale to **evaluate** my progress. If I have reached my goal, I will do something for fun to celebrate.

> *A well-governed appetite is*
> *a great part of liberty.*
> —Seneca

For a disciplined life it is required that we get into a habit of saying "No." If our goal is to live a long healthy life, we have to say "No" to smoking. If our goal is to be trusted by others, we have to say "No" to lying. If we want to lead a moral life, we have to say "No" to hanging out with the wrong crowd. The list goes on and on.

We have an excellent example of how to say "No" in the fourth chapter of Matthew's gospel. The devil tempts Jesus three times to rebel against his Father. And three times Jesus answers with a determined "No." "Get away, Satan. It is written: 'The Lord, your God shall you worship and him alone shall you serve'" (Matthew 4:10). Jesus' mind and heart was set on doing his Father's will and nothing could distract or deter him.

> *Self-respect is the fruit of discipline;*
> *the sense of dignity grows with the*
> *ability to say no to oneself.*
> —Abraham Joshua Herschel

A disciplined life also knows how and when to say a decisive "Yes." If our goal is to become a doctor, we have to say "Yes" to years of study. If our goal is to become a concert pianist, we have to say "Yes" to years of practice. If our goal is to grow in holiness, we have to say "Yes" to prayer. On and on goes this list.

Many people began their day or their week with a "to do" list. As they accomplish each task, they scratch it off their list. I suggest that before we start to write out a "to do" list, we need to first put together a "to think" list. As we stated in chapter three, there is great power in thought.

Once we are clear in our goals and objectives, we need to think about them, keep them frequently before our minds. Having a list of our goals and objectives posted on our bathroom mirror, in front of us on our computer, or visible in our purse or wallet will cause us to think frequently on where we are headed. It helps to often read them out loud. If our thoughts are focused, the necessary actions will follow.

> *Some people regard discipline as a chore. For*
> *me, it is a kind of order that sets me free to fly.*
> —Julie Andrews

Discipline sets us free, free from the demands of our emotions, free from the tyranny of the clock and free from laziness. As we said, discipline involves the tough task of setting priorities, making a plan and following that plan.

We can't do everything people ask of us, nor can we do all the things our hearts would like to accomplish. So we have to make tough choices on the use of our time and talents, and let the rest go.

> *I've... learned that only through focus can*
> *you do world class things, no matter*
> *how capable you are.*
> —Bill Gates

Athletes know the value of discipline. They put in long hours of practice, eat the right food and get enough sleep in order to be in shape to win a game or match. Students know the value of discipline. They sacrifice a lot of fun time in order to study and get good grades.

Christians have the season of Lent for special acts of discipline. We "give up" something that we like, e.g., candy, desserts, movies and TV, in order to be free from inordinate desires and free for acts of charity. Like St. Paul, "I drive my body and train it, for fear that, after having preached to others, I myself should be disqualified" (1 Corinthians 9:27).

> *The art of living consists of knowing which*
> *impulses to obey and which must*
> *be made to obey.*
> —Sidney J. Harris

A disciplined life not only helps us to be more effective and accomplish more, it also brings an inner peace. The techniques of discipline help us to know who we are, where we are going and how to get there. When our goals and objectives are in keeping with God's laws, then discipline is that moral activity that leads to a holy and whole life. The reward is a joy that surpasses all understanding.

> *A good conscience is a continual Christmas.*
> —Benjamin Franklin

Chapter 24

Play

Gladness of heart is the very life of man.
Cheerfulness prolongs his days.
—Sirach 30:22

A late middle-aged man dies and goes up to the Pearly Gates. St. Peter asks his name, and this conversation follows:

Mr. Grey: "My name is Grey. J. R. Grey"

St. Peter: "Hmmm.... Can't seem to find you in our books. Well, no matter. Tell me, Mr. Grey, did you live a good life while you were on earth?"

Mr. Grey: "Oh, yes. I went to school for many years, studied diligently, got good grades, and finally obtained my degree. Then I worked hard for the rest of my life to support my family. I had three children and got them all through college. My wife has a fine home and plenty of insurance. I always supported my church, and gave regularly to the poor. I voted at every election. I was a scout leader. I...."

St. Peter: "Whoa... I just found your summary. It shows a long list of the good deeds you did for your family and community. Now let's see... Must be a page missing. I don't see anything here about you enjoying life."

Mr. Grey: "Well, I was awfully busy. My job was very demanding and I had to put in a lot of overtime. There were a lot of bills, so there was not much time for play. And there were so many requests by groups that needed me. I was a scout leader. I coached little league. I gave blood. I...."

St. Peter: "You mean you didn't take time for fun?

Mr. Grey: "I knew that life was short. There was

so much to do."

St. Peter: "Mr. Grey, God is not going to like my report. The Creator put in a lot of effort crafting a beautiful world for you, a world filled with color and music, fresh air and sunshine, children and flowers and all. He made you in such a way that you could run and dance and frolic and have fun. He certainly expected you to enjoy creation.

"I'm sorry. You are going to have to go back to earth and do your life over again."

This story is certainly a reversal from what many of us were taught. Those of us who grew up in Western civilization were immersed in utilitarian philosophy. This philosophy propounds that in order to be of value a person must be useful. Our self-worth depends on what we accomplish. Moreover, if we grew up in America, we were exposed to the Puritan work ethic: "Don't waste time. Keep your nose to the grindstone. Be responsible. Be productive. Don't be lazy." Many a preacher warned us that idleness is the devil's workshop.

Now and then there was someone who counseled, "All work and no play makes Jack a dull boy." So occasionally we would take "time out" for play. But we did not push it.

> *The people who play are the creators.*
> —Holbrook Johnson

Along with the desire to meet our responsibilities, along with the drive to be productive and of value, there was also the drive to compete. In order to "keep up with the Jones'," we decided to take on a part-time job. And what did this produce? A nation of workaholics. It also produced an abundance of programs to help people cope with stress and burnout.

> *The human person...is only completely a*
> *human person when he or she plays.*
> —Friedrich Schiller

I suggest that we do a reversal. When planning our days many of us put together a "to do" list of people to see, places to go and things to do. A "to do" list is usually a work list. I suggest we reverse that. Let's put play on the top of the list. Before we schedule our work and other responsibilities, we need to schedule our daily, weekly and monthly plans for play, recreation, and leisure.

If this sounds selfish and creates a feeling of guilt, be assured that we are proceeding according to how we are made. For if play comes first, we will be a more alert and energized for our work, more cheerful and pleasant when dealing with people, and more physically and emotionally equipped to meet our responsibilities. Besides, with less stress and burnout, we will most likely live longer and be able to serve our family, our country and our God for many more years. Everybody wins.

> *We do not quit playing because we grow old,*
> *we grow old because we quit playing.*
> —Oliver Wendell Holmes

There is a danger that we can over-organize our playtime. Sometimes the best relaxation is to just slow down and do nothing. Take a stroll, dine slowly, gaze at the stars and grin.

Look at the root word of "recreation." To play is to "re-create", to create anew and to impart fresh life. Like the doctor's slap on the newborn's behind, play wakes us up to life. If we engage in physical play, our bodies are strengthened and made healthier. If we entertain our minds, the imagination is released and new thought processes revealed. If we provide a fun theater for our emotions, new depths of meaning are felt and fresh possibilities are discovered.

*People who cannot find time for recreation
are obliged sooner or later to find time for
illness.*
—John Wanamaker

This is a long and roundabout way of commenting on something Jesus said. "Whoever welcomes this child in my name welcomes me" (Luke 18:2). He was of course talking about welcoming into our lives the powerless and those the world considers unimportant, to love and affirm those who are not in a position to give back.

But maybe we can stretch it a bit to welcome also the little child that lives inside each of us. A child likes to play. To welcome the spirit of play is to welcome a sense of fairness, of innocence and of balance in our lives.

To welcome that spirit of play means we don't worry about who is most important as the apostles sometimes did. As good starting point is to heed the Lord's words to his apostles, "Come away by yourselves to a deserted place and rest a while" (Mark 6:310).

*To be for one day entirely at leisure is
to be for one day an immortal.*
—Chinese proverb

Chapter 25

Understand Suffering

*Jesus was in such agony and he prayed so
fervently that his sweat became like drops
of blood falling on the ground.*
—Luke 22:44

Often we read in the newspaper about a murderer who is
captured and punished, a thief who is sentenced to prison,
or a terrorist who meets death. Quietly we reflect, "Well,
they got what they deserved."

But what about the headlines that tell us of the suffering
of the innocent? The evening news informs us about children
starving in Africa, poor people whose homes were destroyed
by a flood, and a busload of senior citizens killed in an
accident on the highway.

Maybe it's you. You are trying to lead a good life, and
suddenly you come down with a serious illness, or there is
an unexpected death in your family, or you come up against
serious financial difficulties.

*Why me? Why this poor family? Why these children?
Why does God allow this?* People ask me, "Father, you're a
priest. Tell us, why do these things happen?" It's a tough
question. And I can only offer partial answers.

1) I Don't Know
The first reply I give to the question of "why?" is to say, "**I
don't know.**" That may not seem like much of an answer,
but it is realistic. And I am not alone. The apostle Paul,
brilliant theologian that he was, couldn't grasp it all either.

At one point he wrote to his parishioners in Rome, "How inscrutable are God's judgments and how unsearchable his ways" (Romans 11:33). Paul was aware not only of the immense good in the world, but also of the suffering.

Like Paul, our minds are too small to fully comprehend the complex picture of how God acts in this world. I don't believe that God sends down evil upon us. But he seldom suspends the laws of nature. So planes crash, storms occur and people get sick. Nor does God take away people's free will. So we have crimes, injustice, wars, oppression and drunk drivers. People choose to hurt one another.

From all this we easily see that suffering is a "mystery," too deep to understand. But everybody will eventually wrestle with this mystery and we are capable of some insight at times.

2) All Things Work for Good

My second approach to the question is to reflect upon the words of St. Paul to the Romans. "We know that **all things work for good** for those who love God" (Romans 8:28).

Do the innocent suffer? Obviously. Look at Jesus on the Calvary and Mary agonizing along with him. Mary didn't understand the why of it all, but she knew something about how God worked. She knew that God would work something good out of all this. So she waited. She trusted. And then came Easter morning! From death came life.

I have always grown from my problems and challenges.
From the things that don't work out,
that's when I've really learned.
—Carol Burnett

I know a woman who spent her entire life in a wheelchair. Tremendous suffering. But because of her hardship she grew to be one of the wisest and most compassionate persons I ever knew. From death came life. I know a family that had a retarded child. Because of this child, the family grew from selfishness to self-giving. From death came life. An aunt of mine used to speak of the Great Depression during the 1930's. There was much hardship. Yet in her neighborhood people seemed to have time for one another—a community spirit developed. From death came life.

3) No Permanent Home

A third reflection on suffering leads me to this truth. Life is full of reminders that we have here **no permanent home.** To know this, to appreciate this, and to live by this is indeed to have found a hidden treasure that some never find.

That means we won't waste our brief time on earth grasping things that rust away. We will spend our life on the things that outlast it. If suffering hasn't taught us this much, then we are still in first grade in the school of life. To realize that we have here no permanent home helps us to see all suffering from an eternal perspective. There is some peace in that.

4) Baptism

A fourth reflection has to do with the profound implications of **baptism.** *Does suffering seem to you like such a waste? Meaningless? Empty?* Was Christ's suffering and death on the cross a waste, meaningless, and empty? Of course not. It was supremely important for the salvation of the world. Through baptism we are members of the Body of Christ.

When we suffer, in some way it is Christ suffering. And he does not suffer in vain. Our suffering has eternal value in ways that we will never fully understand in this life. How incomprehensible are God's ways that he involves you and me in the saving work of his Son.

Suffering...

- A mystery that boggles our minds.
- The area of life where God draws good out of evil.
- The school where we learn that earth is not our permanent home.
- The Calvary where we join Christ in his saving work.

We can knock on the door of any home and we will find there a person who just had, is having, or will soon have a serious bout with suffering. That means we have daily opportunities to extend compassion and concern. Suffering is at least, and always, a call to love.

Chapter 26

Use Your Power

*The better we feel about ourselves, the fewer
times we have to knock somebody else
down to feel tall.*
—Odetta

*L*et's begin with a riddle. Imagine that over here on my right is a little three-foot tree, and over here on my left is another little three-foot tree. There is a group of people gathered around each tree. As the tree on the right begins to grow, the people pour something over it, and the tree begins to bend over and shrivel up. Each time the tree tries to straighten itself up and start to grow, the people pour something over it and it bends over and shrivels up. This goes on and on, and the little tree remains weak and scrawny and unproductive all throughout its life.

Now, the tree on the left.... When it begins to grow, the people gathered around pour something over it, and the tree quickly brightens up and gets bigger. Time after time these people pour something over the tree and it continues to grow stronger and healthier. Soon its roots go deep, its branches spread out, and it becomes a tall, stately, majestic, towering tree beautiful to behold.

What are these two groups pouring over these trees? The answer is simple. The people on the right are pouring poison, acid, and all sorts of toxic materials, stuff that harms and eventually kills the tree. The people on the left are pouring fertilizer, plant food, fresh water, stuff that helps the tree grow and prosper.

The second riddle is a little more difficult. I'd like you to imagine on my right a little child, and on my left another little child. Both have a group of people gathered around them. The little child on my right tries to grow and develop, but the people pour something over it, and the child bends over and shrivels up. Again the child struggles to straighten up and grow, and again these people pour something over it and it winces, flinches and withdraws. This goes on and on, and the poor child never grows and develops. During its life it remains sick, scrawny, weak and unproductive.

When the child on my left starts to grow, the people gathered around it pour some stuff on it, and it brightens up and grows. The people pour more stuff on the child and it gets healthier and grows some more. They pour more stuff and finally the child becomes strong, beautiful, handsome, fully human and fully alive.

Now the riddle is this. Both groups of people, the ones on the right and the ones on the left, are pouring the same stuff on these children. What is it? The answer: WORDS! Yes, words. But obviously different kinds of words.

> *To speak of 'mere words' is much like*
> *speaking of 'mere dynamite.'*
> —C. J. Ducasse

Words are very powerful. They have the power to kill and they have the power to give life. On the right, the people are pouring words such as these:

> *Get out of my way, dummy.*
> *Don't bother me.*
> *How could you be so stupid?*
> *You never do anything right.*
> *Why can't you be like so-and-so?*
> *You're such a nerd.*
> *I don't have time for you.*
> *You'll never amount to anything.*
> *Why don't you act your age?*

Even worse, they use words and phrases that are racial slurs, ethnic put-downs, along with swear words and phrases that deeply insult and tear down. The result is that the child ends up feeling inadequate, has a poor self-image, lacks self confidence, loses the ability to dream, has difficulty dealing with failure, and is filled with anger, depression, apathy and sadness. The child's life, full of possibilities, never develops. It is doomed to defeat. Needless to say, it has a tough time believing in a loving Creator.

The words that the people on my left are pouring upon the child are words like these.

> *Welcome.*
> *It's so nice to be with you.*
> *You are such fun.*
> *Nice going.*
> *Keep up the good work.*
> *You really tried hard.*
> *You're such a delight.*
> *What do you think?*
> *What are you feeling?*
> *You are such a good friend.*
> *You're beautiful.*
> *I am going to miss you.*
> *You can do it.*
> *Thank you.*
> *I love you.*

Constantly pouring words like these over the child has amazing results. The child grows up with a healthy self-image, has lots of self-confidence, is filled with hope, is able to dream, can deal with failure, wants to share its gifts and talents, and knows how to spread joy. The child grows up feeling a peace within. It senses a deep bond with other human beings, and possesses a real love for God who first gave it the gift of life.

In chapter 25 of the gospel of Matthew, Jesus gives us the parable about the talents. There is a danger in reading this parable. We may see only the obvious lesson about using our talents well, and fail to see how it extends to the talents of others. The parable tells us not to bury our talents. It also implies not to bury the talents of others but to affirm them, encourage them, enable them and help them to grow. All of us possess the life-giving talent to show positive regard to everyone we meet.

> *The greatest good you can do for another is*
> *not just share your riches, but reveal*
> *to them their own.*
> —Benjamin Disraeli

We use the term "mortal sin." What comes to mind are things like murder, adultery, blasphemy, etc. Under mortal sins most would not list such things as insults, hurtful words, unfair criticism and useless faultfinding. In some cases, I would. So many times I have seen negative words squelch initiative, stifle enthusiasm, suffocate creativity, stomp on a self-image, and kill joy. That sure sounds mortal to me.

How many marriages have eventually died because of a finicky, complaining husband or a negative, nagging wife?

How many parish projects or community actions never got off the ground because ideas were belittled or motives misjudged?

How many competent people shy away from running for public office because they fear that they and their family will be treated unfairly by the media?

Yes, words can be lethal. A forked tongue can easily poison another's enthusiasm. Only God knows how many great gifts were never developed, how many great deeds never accomplished because some harping critic buried another's talents with negative words.

On the other hand, there is the hesitant child making all sorts of mistakes on the piano. But someone says, "Keep trying. You can do it. You're making some nice sounds there." His talents blossom and a concert pianist is born.

A young woman wants to become a doctor but fears failure in a man's world. Someone says, "Go ahead. You've got what it takes. I believe in you." And thousands of sick people soon benefit from her skills.

A person is depressed on the job and feels he is not accomplishing much. Then someone says, "Boy, I'm glad you are around here. You really brighten up this place." And he becomes creative and productive once again.

Yes, words can be life-giving. A kind tongue can nourish another's spirit. Only God knows how much good and beauty have come into our world because some industrious and reliable servant took the time and used the right words to make another's talents grow.

Our riddle was about two children. Guess what? We are all children. No matter our age, we all have room to grow and develop and blossom and produce. Each day is precious. Each moment in each day is precious. Why waste time making someone else's life miserable with negative words. We have the opportunity each day to fill the world with uplifting words, patient words, forgiving words, words that bring laughter, words that bring peace, words that make the heart sing, and words that lead to grateful prayer.

Then at the end of our lives, we can look forward to hearing those precious words poured upon us, "Well done, my good and faithful servant. Come, share your Master's joy" (Mathew 25:21).

Chapter 27

Love the Earth

The earth is the Lord's and all it holds,
the world and those who live there.
—Psalm 24:1

I get very upset whenever I see homeless people. They carry with them their meager possessions. They do not eat balanced meals, nor do they have adequate health care. They lack security and often fear for their lives. They do not enjoy family support. They do not have meaningful employment. They have nowhere to lay their heads. It is a sad plight.

For some of the homeless their situation is even sadder because they once had a beautiful home. However, due to neglect, laziness and greed their home was damaged, destroyed or condemned. And now they are out in the cold.

Imagine for a moment not a homeless person but a homeless human race. In the not too distant future, we may lose this beautiful home we call the earth. Due to neglect, laziness and greed, we now have polluted much of our air and water. We are losing farmland, wetlands and forests. Our ozone layer is being depleted. Toxic and nuclear waste is poisoning the environment. Species are disappearing and global warming threatens life everywhere. Our home is burning and our family is dying. We need to do something about it immediately

First we need to go back to the beginning. In the beginning, "God looked at everything he had made, and he found it very good" (Genesis 1:31). Yes, the sun and the moon, the earth and sea, fish and birds, animals and plants, and all human persons—all are very good. And because they are good we need to **love them with a passion.**

> *Love all God's creation, both the whole and every grain of sand. Love every leaf, every ray of light. Love the animals, love the plants, love each separate thing. If thou love each thing thou wilt perceive the mystery of God in all; and when once thou perceive this, thou wilt thenceforward grow every day to a fuller understanding of it until thou come at last to love the whole world with a love that will then be all embracing and universal.*
> —Fyodor Dostoevsky

When we love people, we praise them and let them know how much we admire them. We tell them how much we esteem them and appreciate them.

It is fitting to do the same with the earth. When we reflect on the beauty of our earth-home, we are filled with wonder and awe. And our words of praise turn into a prayer that exalts the Creator of it all.

> *Let the earth bless the Lord; praise and exalt him above all forever. Mountains and hills, bless the Lord; praise and exalt him above all forever. everything growing from the earth, bless the Lord; praise and exalt him above all forever.*
> —Daniel 3:74-76

There are no easy solutions to the ecological challenges of our time. But motivation is the key. Self-preservation has not moved us very far. Guilt has not energized us. Greed had led us down wrong paths. Only love is up to the task.

True love wants to protect the beloved. True love is willing to sacrifice for the good of the beloved. True love wants the beloved not only to survive but to flourish. True love is creative, imaginative, resourceful and ingenious. To love the earth is the only way to save it.

It is important to see ourselves not as separate from the earth but as one with it. We rightly call the earth "Mother Earth," for we depend upon her for our air, water, food, shelter and clothing. The earth provides for us. In protecting and preserving the earth, we achieve oneness with that which sustains our life. This oneness leads to wholeness and delight.

> *Half of our misery and weakness derives from the fact that we have broken with the soil and that we have allowed the roots that bound us to the earth to rot. We have become detached from the earth, we have abandoned her. And a man who abandons nature has begun to abandon himself.*
> —Pierre Van Passen

Where do we find the best plan for caring for creation? Kindergarten!

In his book, *All I Really Need to Know I Learned in Kindergarten,* Robert Fulghum reminds us of what we first learned (or should have learned) as children.

Below is a partial list. Among other things, our parents along with our teachers instructed us to:

1. Play fair.
2. Share everything.
3. Don't hit people.
4. Put things back where you found them.
5. Clean up your own mess.

6. Don't' take things that aren't yours.

7. Say you're sorry when you hurt somebody.

8. Wash your hands before you eat.

9. Flush.

10. Play and work every day.

11. Be aware of wonder.

As regards the earth and its people, these instructions match up with:

1. Education for all. Basic medical care for all. Fair immigration policies.

2. The end of world hunger. World food resources shared with the poor.

3. No war. The end of nuclear weapons.

4. Recycling. Reforestation. Reclamation of surface coal mines.

5. Clean air. Clean streets. The reversal of global warming.

6. Honesty replacing greed.

7. Everyone willing to say "I'm sorry" and "I forgive."

8. Clean water for all.

9. Adequate sanitation for all.

10. Nations sharing musicians, singers, dancers, and comedians as well as teachers, doctors, plumbers, carpenters, etc.

11. National Parks preserved. Museums supported. Star-gazing encouraged.

This is only a partial list. There are many other practical applications of these kindergarten lessons. If little children can learn such lessons and put them into practice, there is no excuse for us adults.

Have you ever noticed how happy kindergarteners are? There is genuine joy that results from playing fair, sharing, not hitting people, etc.

But there is an even more basic reason for their joy. They feel loved.

A child can tell within the first five seconds of the first day of school whether or not it is going to be a good year. They can tell from non-verbal cues whether their teacher likes them or not. If the children experience love from their teacher, they feel safe, are willing to cooperate and look forward to going to school. More importantly, if they know that their parents love them, they feel protected, they feel worthwhile and they have peace.

What qualities do you think a person should have in order to be president, or a senator, a governor or a mayor? What qualities do you think a person should have in order to be pope, or a cardinal, a bishop or a pastor?

Offhand I would say these people should be honest, intelligent, wise and have lots of experience. But something more basic is required.

Have you ever heard a president, a pope, or any other civic or religious leader say, "My people, I love you?" Often? Seldom? Ever?

Love is the most important qualification for all of the above mentioned positions. If a leader possesses a deep commitment of love for his/her people, he/she will instinctively show respect, play fair, clean up, share, tell the truth, not do war, and practice all the rest of those kindergarten rules. He/she will care for the environment where the human race dwells.

When we see someone recycling, planting a tree, or taking medicine and toxic chemicals to a safe dump site, we should hug them. When we see someone protesting nuclear weapons production or voting against extravagant military spending, we should hug them. They are helping us protect our home and our family. They are loving us.

> Every gun that is made, every warship launched, every rocket fired, signifies in the final sense a theft from those who hunger and are not fed, those who are cold and are not clothed.
> —President Dwight Eisenhower (1953)

President Eisenhower was prophetic. It is estimated that it would take about 30 billion dollars to end world hunger for a year. The Pentagon spends that much on average every twenty days. Isn't that fact a wake up call?

> Caring for creation requires a new moral awakening to the compelling demand—clearly articulated in the Bible, expressed in church statements from all major religious denominations, and supported by science—that humans must be stewards of the natural world in order to preserve for ourselves and future generations a beautiful, rich and healthy environment. This is a religious obligation, rooted in a sense of gratitude for creation and reverence for its Creator.
> —Passionist Earth and Spirit Website

Jesus lived upon this earth, was buried in this earth, and rose from this earth. That makes our planet a sacred place, the place of the visitation of our God. Let us take off our shoes. We are walking upon holy ground.

Chapter 28

Know Jesus

*Have I been with you for so long a time
and you still do not know me, Philip?*
—John 14:9

*M*oses Mendelssohn, the great-grandfather of the famous German composer, was not a very handsome man. In fact, he was inflicted with a grotesque humpback.

One day he and his family were visiting a merchant in Hamburg when he noticed the man's beautiful daughter. Moses fell hopelessly in love with her. Unfortunately she was repulsed by his misshapen appearance.

When it was time for him to leave, Moses gathered up all his courage to try to speak with her. But this beautiful girl wouldn't even look at him. And this caused him much pain. After several attempts at conversation, Moses shyly asked, "Do you believe marriages are made in heaven?"

"Yes," she replied—still looking at the floor. "And do you?"

"Yes I do," he replied. "You see, in heaven, at the birth of each boy, the Lord announces which girl he will marry. When I was born, my future bride was pointed out to me. Then the Lord added, 'But your wife will be humpbacked'

"Right then and there I called out, 'Oh, Lord, a humpbacked woman would be a tragedy. Please, Lord, give me the hump and let her be beautiful."

This beautiful girl looked up into his eyes. Then she reached out and touched his hand. Later she became his devoted wife.

The story reminded me of the words of the prophet Isaiah:

It was our infirmities that he bore, our sufferings that he endured.... He was pierced for our offenses, crushed for our sins. Upon him was the chastisement that makes us whole, by his stripes we were healed.
—cf. Isaiah 53

Indeed, Jesus took upon himself the infirmities of us all. We who were once humpbacked with selfishness and sin have been made beautiful by the sufferings and death of this Jesus on the cross.

Who was this Jesus?
What kind of man was he that rough, rugged fishermen dropped their nets to follow him? It is important for us to know him as best we can.

Now this is eternal life, that they should know you, the only true God, and the one whom you sent, Jesus Christ.
—John 17:3

Outdoorsman
Jesus was an **outdoorsman**, a carpenter's son, strong, robust and capable of walking great distances. He had a booming voice that could speak to 5000 people without a microphone. Eventually his strength enabled him to endure scourging, the crowning with thorns and carrying the cross to Calvary.

Gentle Way
Physically very strong, yet Jesus had a **gentle way** with children. When the women brought up their children to see him, the apostles tried to turn them away. But Jesus said, "Let the little children come to me...." Then he put his arms around them and blessed them (cf. Mark 10:13).

Angry?

Did Jesus ever get **angry**? The gospels record one incident when he got angry. When he came upon the men buying and selling in the temple, he became very upset and began tossing them out, knocking over the tables of the money changers. He said, "It is written: 'My house shall be a house of prayer,' but you are making it a den of thicvcs" (Matthew 21:12-13). Nobody fought back.

Cry?

Did Jesus ever **cry**? The gospels record two times when Jesus wept. Once over the city of Jerusalem and once over the death of his friend Lazarus. Jesus experienced genuine grief and shed tears.

Disappointed

Jesus felt **disappointment.** When he cured the ten lepers, only one came back to thank him. He asked, "Where are the other nine" (Luke 17:17)? It must have hurt.

Storyteller

Jesus was a **storyteller**. "Once upon a time, a man had two sons..." (cf. Matthew 21:28). "Once upon a time a woman lost a coin..." (cf. Luke 15:8). "Once upon a time there was a rich man..." (cf. Luke 165:19).

Nature Lover

He **loved nature**, his Father's creation. Jesus' stories and parables often referred to sheep, to seeds, to vines, to the birds of the air and to the lilies of the field....

Compassonate

Jesus experienced **compassion.** He had compassion on the hungry, so he fed them. He had compassion on the sick, so he healed them. He had compassion on the ignorant, so he taught them.

Forgiving

Jesus was in a constant mode of **forgiving.** He forgave the paralytic (cf. Mathew 9:1-7), the woman caught in adultery (cf. John 8: 1-11), and on the cross he forgave the good thief (cf. Luke 23:43) as well as those who were killing him (cf. Luke 23:34). He instructed Peter to forgive seventy-times seven times (cf. Matthew 18:22). And he taught us all to pray, "Forgive us our trespasses, as we forgive those who trespass against us" (Matthew 6:12).

Concern for Mother

On the cross, in his hour of great physical pain, what was he thinking about? His **mother.** Since the one apostle John was there at the foot of the cross, Jesus said, in effect, "John, take care of my mother. Mother, this is now your son" (cf. John 19:27).

Thoughtful Cook

My favorite story takes place after the resurrection. One morning the apostles were out fishing. When they came near the shore they recognized Jesus waiting for them. *What did Jesus do there?* He cooked some fish. Made them breakfast. Almighty God and Savior making **breakfast** for his friends (cf. John 21:1-14)!

What is the bottom line of our life of faith?

Is it to avoid sin? Is it to practice the beatitudes? Is it ministry? Is it prayer, fasting and almsgiving? Is it receiving the Sacraments? It is contemplation?

The bottom line is summed up in words of St. Paul to the Galatians, "I live now not I but Christ lives in me"

(Galatians 2:20). The goal of life is to let Christ into our hearts and have him take over our lives.

That means we think like Christ. We feel like Christ. We speak like Christ. We act like Christ. We love like Christ.

That means we have **compassion**. We show **hospitality**. We **forgive.**

That means we work for **justice**. We show **patience**. We wash feet and **serve** others. That means we focus on doing the **Father's will**, and into the Father's hands we commend our spirit.

Ultimately, our life is not about us. The goal of our life is to manifest Christ. For that to happen we need to get out of the way. We need to invite Jesus in, welcome him in, and ask him to take over our minds, our hearts and our wills. "I live now not I..."

We need to humble ourselves, bow down and admit that without God we can do nothing. We ask, seek, knock and then open ourselves up to receive.

Finally we need to give thanks for all that God does to us and through us. A grateful heart is a peaceful heart.

In the gospel of John, Jesus says, "I have come that they might have life and have it to the full" (John 10:10). With Christ living within us, heaven has already begun. Our joy is complete.

Chapter 29

Celebrate Easter

Why do you seek the living one among the dead?
He is not here, but he has been raised.
—Luke 24:5

*W*e celebrate the Easter Season for fifty days, ending on the feast of Pentecost. Easter is such a central event in our faith that the Church feels we need to reflect on it over and over. To help us reflect I suggest we use a few "what if" questions.

For instance, what if there was **no forgiveness** of sin? Imagine how depressed Peter would have been if, after denying Christ, he was never forgiven for that. He could not get back to being an apostle. He would have been depressed for the rest of his life.

What if, for us, there was no Sacrament of Reconciliation. If we sinned, there was no forgiveness.

Secondly, what if there was a heaven, but after the original sin the gates were barred to all? Only angels could stay. When somebody on earth died, that was it. **No hope** of eternal joy. Death would have the final word.

Thirdly, what if all human suffering was in vain, had no purpose, **no meaning**? Suffering was just a waste of time. Useless pain.

Finally, what if there was **no real purpose** in living. We would just be born, go to school, go to work, have some joys, experience sorrows, try to survive, and then die. What if our lives had no rhyme, reason, or rational goal.

Four *What ifs:*
- No forgiveness of sins.
- No hope of eternal life.
- No meaning to suffering.
- No purpose to living.

Sounds pretty depressing. In the face of all these *What ifs* comes the fact of Easter!

First of all, because Christ died and rose from the dead, there *is* **forgiveness** of sins. Christ nailed our sins to the cross and in his resurrection conquered the power of sin. So Peter and all who have sinned could be reconciled with God. In fact, God even helps us be sorry for our sins, so that we come to him to ask forgiveness.

Second, because Christ died and rose from the dead, death no longer has the last word.

The gates of heaven *are* open and we have **hope** of eternal joy with God. As St. Paul said, "O death, where is your victory? O death, where is your sting" (1 Corinthians 15:55)?

Thirdly, because Christ died and rose from the dead, all our suffering has tremendous **meaning.**

We are baptized into Christ. Our suffering is his suffering and he never suffers in vain. Somehow our pain is Christ's pain and is intimately involved in the salvation of the world.
Finally, because Christ died and rose from the dead, there is **a sublime purpose** to our lives.

We are here so that Christ can live in us, work through us, manifest himself through us, do his work through us and love through us. Whether we express it in raising a family, serving the poor, working for justice, standing up for truth, or setting good example, we are God's instruments. Our purpose is to help bring about the kingdom of God more fully upon this earth.

Christ is alive in us. We can rejoice now and forever!

The only way to cheer yourself up
is to cheer someone else up.
—Mark Twain

Chapter 30

Journey Together

*God is love, and whoever remains in love
remains in God and God in him.*
—1 John 4:16

*P*icture this. A Pakistani policeman is sent to break up a demonstration. He tells an Indian man to get off the street. The man won't. So the policeman pushes him and shoves him until he falls down. Then the policeman beats the man on the head until he becomes unconscious. The Indian lies on the unpaved street, out cold, looking half dead. The policeman just stands there, with little feeling, gazing down upon him.

All of a sudden a chill runs down the policeman's spine. Is this man really an Indian? It looks like he is wearing a mask. The policeman reaches down and, grabbing a corner of what looks like a mask, he pulls it off. And, behold, there before him is the unconscious face of a Chinese person. But wait. That looks like a mask too. The policeman pulls it off. And now he sees the face of an Italian. The policeman again pulls off a mask. And now he is looking at the face of a Mexican. Another mask is pulled off. Now he sees the face of an Arab. The policeman is dumbfounded.

The Arab stirs. His bruised eyes struggle to open. His parched lips part and he begins to speak. He looks up at the policeman and says, "My brother." The policeman says nothing. "My brother," the Arab says, "don't you realize that when you beat that Indian, you beat each and every member of the human family. We are one." Then the man lying on the ground closes his eyes.

The policeman gets nervous. What has he done? What does this mean? While he ponders, he notices that the Arab's face seems to be a mask too. Should he pull it off? What will he see next?

He has to see. He reaches down and pulls. For some reason the mask is more difficult to remove, but he keeps at it. Slowly and carefully, he peels it off. He looks. He gulps. What is going on? How can this be? There is no mistaking the face he sees now. It is his.

Again the man on the ground stirs. His bruised eyes struggle to open. His parched lips part and he begins to speak. He looks up at the policeman and says, "Myself." The policeman says nothing. "Myself, don't you realize that when you beat that Indian, you beat your very self? We are one." And then the man lying in the dust closes his eyes.

Cold sweat starts to run down the policeman's back. He begins to tremble. What has he done? What does all this mean? While he ponders, he notices that the face, *his* face on the beaten man, also looks like a mask. Should he dare to pull it off? What could he possibly see now?

He cannot restrain himself. He must know. So he reaches down and pulls. Now the mask is really difficult to remove, but he keeps at it. Slowly, ever so carefully, he peels it off. He looks. Now he begins to sweat profusely. His face pales. His jaw drops. His eyes are popping out of their sockets. He is looking right at the blood-stained face of Christ.

Christ begins to stir. His bruised eyes struggle to open. His parched lips part and he begins to speak. He looks up at the policeman and says, "My son." The policeman stares, speechless, unable to move. "My son, don't you realize that when you beat these people, you beat me. We are one." The policeman falls to his knees.

Now the bruised and battered Christ struggles to stand up. He gazes out into the horizon. His eyes circle the earth.

He sees countries ravaged by wars, people killed by terrorists, and millions living in political oppression. He sees starving children, homeless families, and battered spouses. He sees innocent babies aborted, teens hooked into drugs, and the elderly neglected.

He sees those struggling to survive with little food, unclean water, no sanitation, no schools. He sees the unemployed, the physically sick, and the emotionally distraught. He sees those who are insulted, and unloved. He sees the fearful, the broken-hearted, and those who feel no hope.

He sees all this and tears stream down his face. His arms reach out, stretching all around the globe and embracing every hurting man, woman, and child. His mouth opens wide and a mighty sound comes forth.

It is a mournful shout, piercing through the night. It ascends the mountains, echoes through the valleys, and rumbles down the streets of every city and village. It bounces across the oceans, thrusts out into outer space and resounds throughout the universe.

The voice of Christ cries out:

These people—this is my body!
And their suffering—this is my blood!

Jesus invites us to come to the altar and eat his body and drink his blood. To receive Communion is to enter into union with the Lord. And with the Lord comes *all* his people. We are one with our Creator's human family, one with its pain and sorrow, one with its hopes and dreams.

When we receive the body and blood of Christ, we receive the **heart of Christ**. Those whom Christ loves become those whom we love.

It takes courage to receive the heart of Christ. But with the heart of Christ beating within us, we will experience as much joy as is possible until we arrive at our eternal home.

> *I have told you this so that my joy may*
> *be in you and your joy may be complete.*
> —John 16:11

Consult not your fears,
But your hopes and your dreams.
Think not about your frustrations,
But about your unfulfilled potential.
Concern yourself not with what you tried and failed,
But with what it is still possible for you to do.
—Pope John XXIII

Chapter End Notes

CHAPTER 1: *Coping with the Blues—the Basics*

[1] For information concerning sleep see: www.nhlbi.nih.gov/about/ncsdr, www.sleepfoundation.org, and www.rd.com/sleep-disorders.

[2] Research has shown that nutrients like the B vitamins, vitamin C, and the mineral selenium convert amino acids from food into mood lifting neurotransmitters. "It's quite clear that even borderline nutrition deficiencies can lead to depression," says Dr. Melvyn Werbach, M.D., author of *Healing through Nutrition,* (Harper Collins, NY, 1993). For information concerning nutrition, see: http://www.nal.usda.gov/fnic/ . For other alternative helps, see: http://www.drdavidwilliams.com/c/mood health recs.asp.

[3] Some issues surface as common sense among nutritionists:

* Too much sugar in food and drinks can give a person a rush of energy, followed by fatigue and an emotional letdown.

* Liquor, like red wine, in moderation can be beneficial, but imbibing too much will dampen spirits (pun intended), especially the next morning. Drinking and driving may result in a serious accident, and that will cause major depression!

* Certain foods seem to have a positive effect on our mood, especially bananas, walnuts, tomatoes and sardines. Medical students who took 2.5 grams of fish oil supplements each day for three months said they felt 20 percent less anxious than those who merely took a placebo.

* In a recent study, *Lactobacillus rhamnosus,* a species of bacteria found in certain yogurts and cheeses, had a calming effect of mice.

[4] Exercise may be just as effective as medication for treating major depression. See the Duke Study: http://www.dukenews.duke.edu/Med/exercise.htm. *How to get started in exercise?* See:http://exercise.about.com/ and www.gymamerica.com.

[5] "More than a hundred studies have confirmed that brisk aerobic exercise such as walking releases clouds of feel-good neurotransmitters in the brain called endorphins. These little molecules make it difficult to experience anxiety, depression malaise or restlessness. The are also powerful boosters of self esteem." Taken from **Supercharge Your Immunity**, by Norman Ford, Prentice Hall, Paramus, NJ, 1998.

And a 1997 study by Dr. Martha Stroandt, reported in the Journal of Gerontology, she found that exercise significantly boosts one's sense of self-confidence, morale, self-esteem and well-being. Her study showed that keeping fit is the least expensive way to lift one's spirits. Another study showed that an added benefit of exercise is a boost in brainpower. Sedentary adults from age 60 to 75 started walking briskly three times a week. They slowly increased their walks from fifteen to forty-five minutes each day they walked. After six months there mental abilities had improved 15%.

[6]To get your mind in the play spirit see: www.gameskidsplay.net/.

[7]Recommended reading: *The Complete Idiot's Guide to Family Games*, by Amy Wall, 2002, Alpha Books, 201 West 103rd St., Indianapolis, IN, 46290.

[8]For further information see: http://www.sada.org.uk/.

[9]For information on full-spectrum lighting and its effect on performance, mood and health, see: www.nrc.ca/irc/fulltext/ir659/contents.html.

Further Reading:
Surviving Depression: A Catholic Approach, by Kathryn Hermes and Sr. K. James Hermes. Pauline Books & Media, 2003.

Healing from Depression: 12 Weeks to a Better Mood, by Douglas Block, M.A. Celestial Arts, Berkley ,CA, 2002.

Protect Us from All Anxiety: Meditations for the Depressed, by William Burke. ACTA Publications. 1998.

How to Heal Depression, co-authored by Harold Bloomfield. Prelude Press, Los Angeles, 1994.

CHAPTER 2: *Accept Reality*

Further Reading:
Overcoming Spiritual Depression, by Arie Elshout and Bartel Elshout. Reformation Heritage Books, 2006.

Self-Coaching: How to Heal Anxiety and Depression, by Joseph J. Luciani, Ph.D. John Wiles and Sons, New York, 2001.

The Noonday Demon: An Atlas of Depression, by Andrew Solomon. Scribner, New York, 2001.

Understanding Depression: A Complete Guide to Its Diagnosis and Treatment, Co-Author: Dr. Donald F. Klein. Oxford University Press, New York., 1994.

Spirituality for Depression, by William A. Burke (audio tape). St. Anthony Messenger Press.

Suggested Websites:

http://www.mayoclinic.com/findinformation/conditioncenters/invoke.cfm?objectid=F61D92BD-C12C-4C1E-98CE1DDC09196EA2

http://www.depressionet.com.au/treatments.html — This site is filled with links to information about a wide variety of treatments, including: Medications, Cognitive Behavioral Therapy (CBT), Electric Convulsive Therapy (ECT), Exercise, Neuro-Linguistic Programming (NLP), Homoeopathy, SAM-e, Sleep, Bright Light Therapy (BLT), Emotional Healing Technique (EFT), Kinesiology, Vitamins, St. John's Wart, and Hypnosis.

http://www.holisticdepression.net/

http://www.freedomfromfear.com/

www.depressionbookstore.com/

CHAPTER 3: *Take Charge of Your Thoughts*

[1]By 1954, more than fifty medical journals had published articles that said the four-minute mile was not humanly possible. Guess what? In 1954 Roger Bannister ran a sub-four-minute mile. Others have done it since. Once you believe or think you can do something, a lot of forces get in line and work with you—concentration, commitment, excitement and confidence.

[2]Did you ever wonder why nations keep fighting wars? Could it be because they, like us, have a large Department of Defense? I can't help but wonder: ***Where is their Department of Peace?***

> *If nations think war, budget for war, build weapons for war, make plans for war, train personnel for war, and expect war, guess what they get? War. If nations would start to think peace, budget for peace, stop selling weapons, make plans for peace, train personnel for peace, and expect peace, guess what might happen? Peace!*

Further Reading:
Emotional Awareness: Overcoming the Obstacles to Psychological Balance, by Dalai Lama and Paul Ekman Ph.D. Henry Holt and Company, New York, 2008.

The Power of Positive Thinking in Business: Ten Traits for Maximum Results, by Scott Ventrella. Free Press, New York, 2001.

The Power of Focus: How to Hit Your Business, Personal and Financial Targets with Absolute Certainty, By Jack Canfield, Mark Victor Hansen, and Les Hewitt. Health Communications, Deerfield Beach, FL, 2000.

Feeling Good: The New Mood Therapy, by David D. Burns, M.D. Avon Books, New York, revised edition, 1999.

CLASSIC: *The Power of Positive Thinking*, by Norman Vincent Peale. Ballantine Books, reissue edition, 1996.

You Can's Afford the Luxury of a Negative Thought, by John Roger and Peter McWilliams. Prelude Press, Los Angeles, CA, 1991.

Suggested Websites:
http://www.rebt.org/essays/depress.html

CHAPTER 4: *Talk to or Communicate with Someone*

[1]Barbara Crow is the past president of the National Association for Music Therapy.

Suggested Reading:
The Dance of Connection: How to Talk to Someone When You're Mad, Hurt, Scared, Frustrated, Insulted, Betrayed, or Desperate, by Harriet Lerner. Harper Collins, 2001.

Beyond Talk Therapy: Using Movement and Expressive Techniques in Clinical Practice, edited by Daniel J Wiener, Ph.D. American Psychological Association, Washington, DC, 1999.

Suggested Websites:
http://www.musictherapy.org — Resource for music that heals.

http://www.metanoia.org/imhs/ — Therapists online.

http://helping.apa.org/find.html — To find a psychologist.

http://www.lifejournal.com/resources.html — Resource for journal writing.

http://www.poetrytherapy.org/links/poetry_sites.htm — Resource for poetry that heals.

CHAPTER 5: *Listen*

[1]Rhea Zakich is the creator of the *Ungame*, an excellent tool for encouraging communication. Rhea came up with the game because of a serious illness. She went to a doctor about a sore throat. As it turned out, it was more than a sore throat. It was a very serious an ailment, nodules on

her vocal chords. The doctor instructed her not to speak for a month. Just write notes when she had to. Otherwise she would lose her voice forever. This woman went home, determined to follow the doctor's orders. She quickly got into the habit of writing instructions, requests, notes of thanks, etc., to her family

But not being able to say anything out loud she had time to listen to her family—and wonder. So she began writing them notes asking them questions on a deeper than usual level. "What are your favorite songs?" "What would you do if you had a million dollars?" "What is your biggest fear?" On and on the questions came. Her knowledge and understanding of her husband and children became rich and deep. Eventually she marketed a boardgame the **Ungame** with cards with value questions. Now other families could have something of the learning experience she had. Visit her website: http://www.rheazakich.com/

[2]I would like to offer the following exercise to sharpen listening skills: Begin by quieting the noise *without.* This involves setting aside a regular time each day to be quiet. Then find or make a quiet place, where there is no TV, radio, or newspaper. If possible get away from street noise, and the sound of people. The second step is to quiet the noise *within.* Push aside all cares, worries and fears for the time being. This is basic thought control. Walk slowly to your quiet place. Then begin:

- On a **first** day read something (a favorite bible selection, a piece of poetry) and read it leisurely, meditatively. Linger on words and phrases.

- On a **second** day listen to some soft music. Feel it. Absorb it. Sway.

- On a **third** day, take along some pictures of beautiful artwork. Stare. Savor.

- On a **fourth** day, take nothing along. Stand for a while and give your attention to your breathing. Sit for a while and focus on your heartbeat. Then lie down for a while and...just be. And smile.

- On a **fifth** day, take nothing along. If your quiet place is outdoors, turn your senses to nature all around you. Take all the time you need to see the trees and flowers, hear the birds and crickets, smell the fresh air, and feel the wind at your face and the ground at your feet. Touch the grass. No thoughts. Just be in your place on this planet, in this universe. (If you are indoors, imagine yourself in some beautiful setting. Reflect on how it would feel to be there right now.)

- Finally, on a **sixth** day, take along a photo of someone you love. Gaze at them. Think about them. Care for them. Experience the love deeply. Be grateful.

> *Then I want to sit and listen and have someone talk, tell me things—their life histories —books they have read, things they have done —new worlds! Not to say anything— to listen and listen and be taught.* —Anne Morrow Lindberg

Further Reading:

Are You Really Listening? Keys to Successful Communication, by Paul J. Donoghue, Ph.D. And Mary E. Siegel, Ph.D. Ave Maria Press, Soren Books, Notre Dame, IN, 2005.

A Heart to Listen: Learning to Become a Listening Person, by Michael Mitton. Bible Reading Fellowship, 2004.

How to Get Your Husband to Talk to You, by Nancy Cobb and Connie Grigsby. Multnomah, Sisters, OR, 2001.

Why Men Don't Listen and Women Can't Read Maps, by Barbara and Allan Pease. Random House, New York, 2000.

Listening: The Forgotten Skill: A Self-Teaching Guide (Wiley Self-Teaching Guides) by Madelyn Burley Allen (Wiley Self-Teaching Guides). John Wiley & Sons, 1995.

Men Are from Mars, Women Are from Venus: A Practical Guide for Improving Communication and Getting What You Want in Your Relationships, by John Gray. Harper Collins, 1992.

Listening: God's Word for Today, by Basil Pennington. Continuum, New York, 2000.

You Just Don't Understand, by Deborah Tannen, Ph.D. William Morrow and Co., New York, 1990.

Suggested Websites:

Rhea Zakich is the creator of the "Ungame," an excellent tool for encouraging communication. Visit: http://www.talicor.com/ungame.html.

http://www.listen.org/pages/listening_hall_of_fame.html

CHAPTER 6: *Anger Management*

Further Reading:

Transforming our Painful Emotions: Spiritual Resources in Anger, Shame, Grief, Fear and Loneliness, by James D.Whitehead and Evelyn Eaton Whitehead. Orbis Books, 2010.

Managing Anger: A Handbook of Proven Techniques, by Mitchell Messer. Mitch Messer's Anger Institute, Chicago, 2001.

Anger-Free: Ten Basic Steps to Managing Your Anger, by W. Doyle Gentry. Harper, New York, 2000.

The Angry Self: A Comprehensive Approach to Anger Management, by Miriam M. Gottlieb, Ph.D. Zeig, Tucker, and Theisen Publisher, Phoenix, AZ, 1999.

Make Anger Your Ally, by Neil Clark Warren, Ph.D. Tyndale House Publishers, Wheaton, IL, 1993.

Fire in the Belly, by Sam Keen. Bantam Books, New York, 1991.

Suggested Websites:

http://www.apa.org/pubinfo/anger.html

http://www.angermgmt.com/

http://www.mentalhelp.net/psyhelp/chap7/

CHAPTER 7: *Conquer Fear*

[1]One of my favorite stories on courage comes from the book, *Profiles in Courage,* by John F. Kennedy. In chapter six we read about Mr. Edmond Ross. He was a senator in the critical year of 1868. It was critical because the president of that time, Andrew Johnson, was up for impeachment. Athought there were eleven articles of impeachment, eight of the articles centers around the dismissal of Edwin Stanton, the Secretary of War, and the appointment of a new Secretary of War in violation of the Tenure of Office Act.

Suffice it to say that in 1868 Edmond Ross was being pressured by his party and his constituents to vote in favor of impeachment. However, like all the senators, he took an oath to do impartial justice. So he tried his best to ignore the pressure and vote his conscience. After excruciating analysis of the controversy and profound soul searching, Ross voted his conscience.

Ross, along with six other senators of his party, voted against impeachment. Ross's vote was the tiebreaker. He voted, knowing full well it would be his political downfall. He later wrote. "I almost literally looked down into my open grave. Friendships, position, fortune, everything that makes life desirable to an ambitious man were about to be swept away by the breath of my mouth, perhaps forever."

An editorial from his home state called him "poor, pitiful shriveled wretch". Others in his party referred to him as "the traitor Ross". Still others considered association with him "disreputable and scandalous, and passed him by as if he were a leper." A Justice of the Kansas Supreme Court wrote him, "the rope with which Judas Iscariot handed himself is lost, but (a former Senator's) pistol is at your service."

History vindicated Edmond Ross. Many years later the newspapers and political leaders who had bitterly denounced him were to praise him for his courageous stand. One historian referred to him as the man who performed "the most heroic act in American history, incomparably more difficult than any deed of valor upon the field of battle."

John F. Kennedy summed up his book with this observation. "In whatever area of life one may meet the challenge of courage, whatever may be the sacrifices one faces if he follows his conscience—the loss of his friends, his fortune, his contentment, even the esteem of his fellow people – each must decide for himself or herself the course they will follow. The stories of past courage can define that ingredient—they can teach, the can offer hope, they can provide inspiration. But they cannot supply courage itself. For this each must look into their own soul."

Further Reading:

CLASSIC: *Profiles in Courage*, by John F. Kennedy (1955). Harper Perennial, New York, reissue, 2000.

The Mystery of Courage, by William Ian Miller, Harvard University Press, 2000.

From Panic to Power: Proven Techniques to Calm Your Anxieties, Conquer Your Fears, and Put You in Control of Your Life, by Lucinda Bassett, Harper Collins, 1995.

Feel the Fear and Do It Anyway, by Susan Jeffers, Ph.D. Fawcett Books, reissue, 1992.

Anxiety, Phobias, and Panic: Taking Charge and Conquering Fear, by Reneau Peurifoy. Life Skills, Citrus Heights, CA, 1992.

Anxiety and Panic Attacks, the Cause and the Cure: The Five Point Life – Plus Program for Conquering Fear, by Robert Handly. Rawson Associates, New York, 1985.

CHAPTER 8: *Know Your Inner Truth*

[1]For Ziggy and for us, the feeling of inferiority may be the result of a long history of the words we've heard. See Chapter 26 for further reflection.

[2]Early in his career George Gershwin wasn't doing very well, struggling along on $35.00 a week. Irving Berlin, who was already famous and well established, recognized Gershwin's talents and offered him a job as his musical secretary at three times what he was making writing songs.

Then, in an amazing bit of advice, Berlin told Gershwin not to accept the offer he just made. "If you do", he continued, "you may develop into a second-rate Irving Berlin. But if you insist on being yourself, someday you will become a first-rate George Gershwin." Gershwin accepted Berlin's sound insight and advice, and the rest is history.

Further Reading:

The Art of Extreme Self-Care 2-CD: Transforming Your Life One Month at a Time, by Chreyl Richardson Audiobook, CDHay House; Abridged edition, 2009.

Breaking the Chain of Low Self-Esteem, by Marilyn J. Sorensen, Ph. D. Wolf Publishing Companyh, 2nd edition, 2006.

True Self-esteem: Precious In The Eyes Of God, by Jim McManus. Ligouri, 2005.

Breaking Free from a Negative Self Image: Finding God's true reflection when your mirror lies, by Linda Mintle. Siloam, 2002.

Self-Knowledge and the Self, by David Jopling. Routledge, New York, 2000.

Self-Esteem Enhancers: Inner Directed Guidelines for Successful Living, by Virgie M. Binford, Dorothy N. Cowling. Providence House, Franklin, TN, 1999.

How to Raise Your Self–Esteem, by Nathaniel Branden. Bantam Publications, New York, 1998.

Loving Yourself More: 101 Meditations for Women, by Virginia Ann Froehle, R.S.M. Ave Maria Press, Notre Dame, IN, 1993.

On the Way to Self-Knowledge, by Jacob Needleham and Dennis Lewis. Knopf, New York, 1990.

Suggested Websites:

The National Association of Self-Esteem: http://www.self-esteem-nase.org/

To boost the self-esteem of others: http://www.self-esteemcards.com

Instruments for greater self-knowledge: http://www.personality.cc/mbti.htm

For reflections on self-esteem:
http://www.oprah.com/postcards/omag/200103/omag_200103_postcard.html

CHAPTER 9: *Learn from Life*

[1]If you're a bright person who occasionally does dumb things, I suggest the book, *The 176 Stupidest Things Ever Done*, by Ross and Kathryn Petras. Doubleday, New York, 1996. This book will make you look brilliant.

[2]See the CLASSIC book: *Seven Habits of Highly Successful People*, by Steven Covey.

Further Reading:
Failing Forward: Turning Mistakes into Stepping Stones for Success, by John C. Maxwell. Thomas Nelson, 2007.

Broken Minds: Hope for Healing When You Feel Like You're "Losing It" by Steve Bloem and Robyn Bloem. Kregel Publications, 2005.

Full Catastrophe Living: Using the Wisdom of Your Body and Mind to Face Stress, Pain, and Illness, by Jon Kabat-Zinn. Dell Publishing, 1991.

Coping with Failure, by Norbert Greinacheer and Norbert Mette. Trinity Press International, Philadelphia, 1990.

Suggested Website:
To help children learn from experience, visit:
http://www.nncc.org/SACC/sac25_cope.fail.html

CHAPTER 10: *Deal with Criticism*

Further Reading:
Bullycide: Death at Playtime, by Neil Maar and Tim Field. Bewrite Books, 2011.

Bully in Sight: How to Predict, Resist, Challenge and Combat Workplace Bullying, by Tim Field. Available at:
http://www.successunlimited.co.uk/books/index.htm

Words that Sting: How to Handle Destructive Criticism like Jesus, by John N. Strange IV. CreateSpace, 2011.

CHAPTER 11: *Handle Grief*

Further Reading:
CLASSIC: *On Death and Dying*, by Elisabeth Kubler-Ross, M.D. Scribner, reissue 1997.

Coping with Loss: Praying Your Way to Acceptance, by Carol Luebering. St. Anthony Messenger Press, 2009.

And Jesus Wept, by Andre Mathieu, C.P. 2 CD Audio Book, Passionist Press, 2007.

As You Grieve: Consoling Words from Around the World, by Aaron Zerah. Sorin Books, 2001.

How to Survive the Loss of a Love, by Melba Colgrove, Ph.D., Harold Bloomfield, M.D., & Peter McWilliams. Prelude Press, Los Angeles CA, 1991.

Living with an Empty Chair—A Guide Through Grief, by Dr. Roberta Temes. New Horizon Press, 1992.

Praying our Goodbyes, Joyce Rupp, OSM. Ave Maria Press, Notre Dame, IN, 1988.

Suggested Websites:
http://www.griefnet.org/resources/index.html

http://www.grief-recovery.com/ArticleIndex.html

CHAPTER 12: *Forgive & Be Forgiven*

1) According to Fred Luskin, a Stanford University psychologist, "Holding on to hurts and nursing grudges wears you down physically and emotionally." "Forgiving someone can be a powerful antidote."

In 2001 there was a survey of 1423 adults by the Institute for Social Research of the University of Michigan. This survey found that people who had forgiven someone in their past reported being in better health than others who hadn't. (Cf. Reader's Digest, March 2002, p. 173, "The Healing Power of Forgiveness.")

Further Reading:
Facing Forgiveness: A Catholic's Guide to Letting Go of Anger and Welcoming Reconciliation, by Loughlan Sofield, Carroll Juliano and Gregory Aymond. Ave Maria Press, 2007.

Rooted in Jesus: Healing Generational Defects, by Patricia McLaughlin. Queenship Publishing, Santa Barbara, CA, 2002.

Forgive for Good: A Proven Prescription for Health and Happiness, by Dr. Fred Luskin. Harper, San Francisco, 2001.

The Art of Forgiving, by Lewis Smedes. Moorings, a division of Random House, Nashville, TN, 1996.

The Forgiveness Factor: Stories of Hope in a World of Conflict, by Michael Henderson. Grosvenor Books, London, 1996.

Healing Life's Hurts, by Dennis Linn, Sheila Linn, and Matthew Linn. Paulist Press, 1988.

Making Peace with your Parents, by Harold Bloomfield, Ph. D. Ballentine Books, New York, 1985.

Suggested Websites:
http://www.journeytowardforgiveness.com/

http://www.forgiveness-institute.org/
http://www.ifor.org/

http://www.forgivenessday.org/learning_to_forgive.htm

CHAPTER 13: *Commit Yourself*

1) Statistics tell us that one out of two marriages end in divorce. *Why? Didn't the bride and groom know what they said at the altar? Didn't they mean what they said?*

When we were quite young, most of us learned the words of the standard wedding vows. We took them for granted and grew up knowing what they meant. Or did we? "Do you take this woman as your lawful wife, to have and to hold, from this day forward, for better or for worse, for richer or for poorer, in sickness and in health, until death do you part?" "Do you take this man…?" What bold, challenging, and daring words! These words mean: Do you love this person completely, absolutely, unconditionally, infinitely and forever? Do you commit yourself to him with all your heart, with all your soul, with all your mind, with all your body, and with all your will? Do you choose her, devote yourself to her, covenant yourself to her, and give yourself to God for her? Do you dedicate yourself to his happiness and to his holiness, to his health and to his wholeness? Are you willing to climb the highest mountain for her, and swim the deepest ocean for her? Are you willing to take on all challenges to make you marriage work, to work with all your strength to overcome all obstacles, and not let anyone or anything come between you? Is he the most precious person in your life? Do you desire to grow and be, not just better, but the best man possible for her, the most loving and the most loveable man for her? If called upon, are you willing to give your life for her? If your commitment is not 1000%, don't proclaim, "I do." It won't work. And you are wasting each other's time.

(2)For the complete text see: http://www.huna.org/html/cpestes.html.

Further Reading:
CLASSIC: *Man's Search for Meaning*, by Viktor Frankl. Washington Square Press, revised and updated, 1998.

Common Fire: Leading Lives of Commitment in a Complex World, by Laurent A. Daloz, Cheryl H. Keen, James P. Keen, Sharo Parks, Sharon Daloz Parks. Beacon Press, 1997.

Adult Commitment. An Ethics of Trust, by Elizabeth Willems. University of Press of America, Lanham, MD, 1990.

Commitment: Key to Christian Maturity, by Susan Muto. Paulist Press, New York, 1990.

CHAPTER 14: *Use Your Head*

Further Reading:
CLASSIC: *The Intellectual Life*, by Antonin Sertillanges. Newman Press, Westminster, MD, 1948.

CLASSIC: *The Closing of the American Mind*, by Allan Bloom. Simon and Schuster, N.Y., 1988.

Brain-Based Learning in the Digital Age, by Marilee Sprenger. Association for Supervision & Curriculum Development, 2010.

The New Dictionary of Cultural Literacy: What Every American Needs to Know, by E.D. Hirsh Jr., Joseph F. Kett, and James Trefil. Houghton Mifflin Harcourt, 2002.

Suggested Websites:
http://books.mirror.org/gb.home.html — Great Books

http://www.nytimes.com/learning/

http://www.eb.com/

http://www.inetlibrary.com/

http://www.barnesandnobleuniversity.com

http://www.health-o-rama.org/superlearning/

CHAPTER 15: *Nourish Your Soul*

Further Reading:
CLASSIC: *The Decline of Pleasure,* by Walter Kerr. Simon and Schuster, 1962.

The Heart Aroused: Poetry and the Preservation of the Soul in Corporate America, by David Whyte. Currency Books, revised edition, 2002.

Care of the Soul: A Guide for Cultivating Depth and Sacredness in Everyday Life, by Thomas Moore. HarperPerennial, reprint edition, 1994.

Suggested Websites:
http://www.nga.gov/collection/collect.htm — Art

http://www.bc.edu/bc_org/avp/cas/fnart/arch/ — Architecture

http://dir.yahoo.com/Arts/Humanities/Literature/Poetry/

http://www.classicalarchives.com — Seventeen-thousand-plus classical selections

CHAPTER 16: *Ah! The Turning Point*

[1]There is a true story about a man named Alfred. Alfred lived over a hundred years ago. He was a chemist, an engineer, and an inventor. He was fluent in five languages. And although he was Swedish, he owned large holdings in the oil fields in Russia. So he built up an immense fortune. Well, one day someone mistakenly heard that Alfred has died, and an obituary notice appeared in the paper. Alfred, who hadn't died yet, read his premature obituary, and didn't like what it said. Despite his many skills, the obituary related a rather empty life. So Alfred decided to change his life. And, among other things he decided to leave the bulk of his fortune for an annual reward, a very prestigious award that would encourage others to improve human life in the fields of physics, chemistry, medicine, literature, and peace. To this day the Alfred Nobel prize inspires many people to do great things. The real obituary had some very nice things to say about this millionaire turned philanthropist.

> *All who joy would win must share it.*
> *Happiness was born a twin.*
> —Lord Byron

Further Reading:
CLASSIC: *Love and Will*, by Rollo May. Delacorte Press, reissue ed., 1995.

The Power of Giving, by Azim Jamal and Harvey McKinnon. Jaico Publishing House, Mumbai, India, 2006.

The Power of Kindness: The Unexpected Benefits of Leading a Compassionate Life, by Peiro Ferrucci. Tarcher/Penguin, 2006.

Suggested Websites:
http://www.cnvs.org — Catholic Network of Volunteer Service

http://wwwpalloticenter.org

http://www.JesuitVolunteers.org/

http://networkforgood.org/ —Lists nearly 850,000 charities plus thousands of volunteering opportunities.

http://www.peacecorps.gov/indexf.cfm

http://www.americorps.org/

www.kindness.usetoday.com — www.sharing.usatoday.com

http://www.ysa.org/ — Youth Service America

http://www.volunteermatch.org

http://www.earthwatch.org

http://www.aarp.org/makeadifference/

http://www.oprah.com/postcards/omag/200012/mag_200012_postcard.html — For thoughts on generosity.

CHAPTER 17: *Go to Work*

[1]For the last group, I offer the following inspirational meditation:

> **Strange Prints in the Sand**
> *One night I had a wondrous dream,*
> *One set of footprints there was seen.*
> *The footprints of my precious Lord,*
> *But mine were not along the shore.*
>
> *But then some stranger prints appeared.*
> *I asked the Lord, "What have we here?*
> *Those prints are large and round and neat,*
> *But, Lord, they are too big for feet.*

"My child," he said in somber tone,
"For miles I carried you alone.
I challenged you to walk in faith.
But you refused and made me wait.

You disobeyed. You would not grow.
The walk of faith you would not know.
So I got tired. I got fed up.
And there I dropped you on your butt.

You see, in life, there comes a time
When people must fight, and people must climb.
When people must rise, and people must stand,
Or leave their butt prints in the sand.
　　　　　—Sam Glenn

Further Reading:

Spirituality @ Work.: 10 Ways to Balance Your Life on the Job, by Gregory Pierce. Loyola Press, Chicago, 2001.

Dignity at Work, by Randy Hodson. Cambridge University Press, 2001.

Selling the Work Ethic: From Puritan Pulpit to Corporate PR, by Sharon Beder. Zed Books, 2001.

If Aristotle Ran General Motors: The New Soul of Business, By Thomas Morris. Holt Paperbacks, 1998.

Suggested Websites:

http://bapaxchristi.freeservers.com/dignity_of_workers.htm (article)

http://www.career-lifeskills.com/products_services/atpr/sii/ (services)

http://www.ivillage.com/work (services)

CHAPTER 18: *Laugh*

[1]Please help me expand this list. Send your suggestions to: yes2life@prodigy.net

[2]If you view the movie "Patch Adams," you will observe some creative approaches to get people laughing in a hospital setting.

[3]If you want a Ph.D. to prescribe the above, visit Dr. Steven M. Sultanoff's delightful website: www.humormatters.com and www.RxLaughter.org.

[4]For information on laughter as good exercise, visit: www.LiveScience.com

Further Reading:

A MOM'S LIFE: The Great, the Bad, & the Disgusting, by Brooke Nightingale. *Spirit of Hope Publishing*, Irvine, CA 2011.

Laughing with God: Humor, Culture, and Transformation, by Gerald A. Arbuckly, Forward by Jean Vanier. Liturgical Press, 2008.

Laughter, the Best Medicine. A Laugh-Out-Loud Collection. Reader's Digest, Pleasantville, NY, 2008.

Almost Home: Embracing the Magical Connection Between Positive Humor & Spirituality, by Jacki Kwan, Cameo Publications, 2002.

Compassionate Laughter: Jest for the Health of It, by Patty Wooten, R.N. Jest Press, June, 2002.

Laughter the Best Medicine: The Healing Powers of Happiness, Humor and Joy! by Robert Holden. Thorsons, Harper Collins, London, 1999.

Laffirmations, 1001 Ways to Add Humor to Your Life and Work, by Joel Goodman. Health Communications Inc., 1995.

The Healing Power of Humor: Techniques for Getting Through Loss, Setbacks, Upsets, Disappointments, Difficulties, Trials, Tribulations, and All That, by Allen Klein, Penguin Putnam Inc., 1989.

Suggested Websites:

The American Association for Therapeutic Humor at: www.aath.org

The Humor Project at: www.humorproject.com

Become a Laugh Therapist at: http://worldlaughtertour.com/

http://www.rd.com/content/enhance-your-sense-of-humor/1/ — 19 suggestions from Reader' Digest on how to put humor to your life.

www.cbs.com/latenight/lateshow —Top Ten list from David Letterman

Also see: www.funny2.com http://chrystalinks.com/laughter2.html

CHAPTER 19: *Have a Dream*

Further Reading:

There Are No Limits, by Danny Cox. Executive Book, 2006.

How Youth Can Succeed!: Transforming Dreams into Reality for Young Adults, by Sean C. Stephenson. S. C. S. Publications, 2000.

Suggested Websites:

http://www.tonyrobbins.com/ Personal Power II: The Driving Force Program, by Tony Robbins

CHAPTER 20: *What About Money?*

Further Reading:
America Mania, When More is Not Enough, by Peter C. Wyhbrow, M.D. W. W. Norton & Company; 1ST edition, January 2005.

Illuminated Life, by Joan Chittister, OSB. Published by Orbis Books, 2000.

Becoming Human, by Jean Vanier. Paulist Press, 1998.

How Much is Enough? The Consumer Society and the Future of the Earth, by Alan Durning. Published by Worldwatch Institute, 1992.

Suggested Websites:
http://www.thegoodsteward.com/

http://www.catholicstewardship.org/

CHAPTER 21: *Be Grateful*

[1]Reported by Fred Bauer, Health Communications, Inc.

Further Reading:
Uncommon Gratitude: Alleluia for All That Is, by Joan Chittister and Rowan Willaims. Liturgical Press, March, 2010.

Thanks! How Practicing Gratitude can Make You Happier, by Robert Emmons Mariner Books; Reprint edition, November, 2008.

365 Thank Yous: The year a simple Act of Daily Gratitude Changed my Life, by John Kralik, Hyperion, New York. 2010.

14,000 Things to Be Happy About (Items, places, moods, thoughts, celebrations, and our daily bread) by Barbara Ann Kipfer. Workman Publishing Company, New York. Revised and updated, 2007.

From Resentment to Gratitude, by Henri Nouwen. Franciscan Herald Press, Chicago, 1974.

Grateful Heart (audio), by David Steindl-Rast. Sounds True, 1997.

Suggested Websites:
http://www.momof9splace.com/declare.html — The first National Thanksgiving Proclamation.

http://www.cyberstory.com/CyberStoryText2/ALotToBeStories.html — Stories of gratitude.

CHAPTER 22: *Be a Friend*

Further Reading:
Walking Together: Discovering the Catholic Tradition of Spiritual Friendship, by Mary DeTurris Poust. Ave Maria Press, 2010.

Becoming Friends: Worship, Justice, and the Practice of Christian Friendship, by Paul Wadell. Brazos Press, 2002.

CHAPTER 23: *Take Control*

Further Reading:
The Purpose Driven Life, by Rick Warren. Zondervan, 2011.

A Lifetime of Observations and Reflections On and Off the Court, by John Wooden. Contemporary Publishing Group, 1997.

Awaken the Giant Within, by Anthony Robbins. Free Press, 1992.

CHAPTER 24: *Play*

Suggested Websites:
www.aath.org — Association for Applied and Therapeutic Humor

www.leadinghomecare.com — For audio CD, *Taking What You Do Seriously, but Yourself Lightly,* by Dr. Ann Weeks.

To receive a free weekly humor newsletter titled, *Weeks of Fun*, write: annweeks@insightbb.com.

CHAPTER 25: *Understand Suffering*

Further Reading:
Tattoos on the Heart, The Power of Boundless Compassion, by Gregory Boyle. Free Press, New York, 2010.

The Journey to Peace: Reflections on Faith, Embracing Suffering, and Finding New Life, by Joseph Cardinal Bernardin. Reissue, Doubleday, New York, 2001.

Redemptive Suffering: Understanding Suffering, Living With It, Growing Through It, by William O'Malley. Crossroads, New York, 1997.

Death and Hope, by Harry J. Cargas and Ann White. Corpus Books, New York, 1971.

CHAPTER 26: *Use Your Power*

Further Reading:
The Power of Words and the Wonder of God, General Editors, John Piper & Justin Taylor, Crossway Books, 2009.

Power of Our Words, The: Teacher Language That Helps Children Learn, by Paula Denton. Northeast Foundation for Children, Inc., 2007.

CHAPTER 27: *Love the Earth*

Further Reading:
Unwarranted Influence: Dwight D. Eisenhower & the Military-Industrial Complex, by James Ledbetter. Yale University Press, 2011.

When the Rivers Run Dry: Water—The Defining Crisis of the Twenty-First Century, by Fred Pearce. Beacon Press, 2007.

CLASSIC: *Silent Spring, by Rachel Carson*, 1962. Houghton Mifflin Company, Anniversary edition, 2002.

Pray Always & Never Loose Heart. International Catholic Stewardship Council, Inc. 1998.

Suggested websites:
http://www.earthandspiritcenter.org/resources.htm#greatwork
http://www.earthcharterinaction.org/content/
http://www.usccb.org/sdwp/ejp
http://environment.harvard.edu/religion/main.html
http://asi.newamerica.net/

CHAPTER 28: *Know Jesus*

Further Reading:
A Lenten Journey with Jesus Christ and St. Paul of the Cross, by Victor Hoagland, C.P. Christus Publishing, Wellesley, MA., 2010.

The Gospel of Matthew, by Donald Senior, C.P. Audio CD. Now You Know Media, 2008.

Jesus, A Gospel Portrait, by Donald Senior, C.P. Paulist Press, 1992.

The Jesus Myth, by Andrew Greeley. Doubleday, 1972.

CHAPTER 29: *Celebrate Easter*

Further Reading:

CLASSIC: *New Horizons*, chapter 5, *The Power of His Resurrection,* by Barnabas Ahern, C.P. Fides, 1966.

CLASSIC: *In the Redeeming Christ*, by F. X. Durwell. Sheed and Ward, 1963.

CHAPTER 30: *Journey Together*

Further Reading:

Our Hearts at Sunday Mass, by Alan Phillip, C.P. Spirit of Hope Publishing, Irvine, CA, 2009.

The Language of God, by Francis S. Collins. Free Press, New York, 2007.

That All May Be One, by Ernest Falardeau. Paulist Press, 1999.

Forgotten Truth: The Common Vision of the World's Religions, by Huston Smith. HarperOne, 1992.

Checklist

1) _____ I do the basics:
   _____ I eat a balanced diet.
   _____ I exercise.
   _____ I get enough sleep.
   _____ I play.
   _____ I get plenty of light.

2) _____ I accept the reality of daily troubles.

3) _____ I take charge of my thoughts.
   _____ I focus on positive thoughts.

4) _____ I talk to someone when I am down.

5) _____ I listen to others.

6) _____ I manage my anger.

7) _____ I conquer my fear.

8) _____ I accept the truth of who I am.
   _____ I speak the truth at all times.

9) _____ I learn from life.

10) _____ I handle criticism leveled at me.
    _____ I criticize carefully, and only if necessary.

11) _____ I handle grief.

12) _____ I forgive others.
_____ I forgive myself.

13) _____ I make firm commitments.

14) _____ I am constantly growing in knowledge.
_____ I read and keep informed.
_____ I converse with intelligent people.

15) _____ I feed my soul with beauty:
_____ Art
_____ Music
_____ Silence
_____ Pets
_____ Other

16) _____ I focus my concern on others.
_____ I pray for everyone.

17) _____ I work.
18) _____ I laugh.
_____ I make others laugh.

19) _____ I have a dream.
My dream(s) _____
_____
_____

20) _____ I keep money in perspective.

21) _____ I am grateful.

22) _____ I am a good friend.

23) _____ I am disciplined.

24) _____ I take time to R & R.

25) _____ I believe some good will come from my suffering.

26) _____ I use words to build up and not to tear down.

27) _____ I care for our planet.

28) _____ I believe I am loved by God.

29) _____ I believe in life after death.

30) _____ I believe I am forgiven.

The source of Christian joy is the certainty of being loved by God, loved personally by our Creator, by the One who holds the entire universe in his hands and loves each one of us and the whole great human family with a passionate and faithful love, a love greater than our infidelities and sins, a love which forgives.
Benedict XVI

About the Author

Father Alan Phillip, C.P, is a Catholic priest and member of the Passionist Religious Congregation. He received his Masters of Divinity from St. Meinrad School of Theology in St. Meinrad, Indiana, and has pursued further theological studies at the Catholic Theological Union in Chicago, Illinois.

Since his ordination in 1967, Fr. Alan has served as Associate Pastor at Immaculate Conception parish in Chicago, Illinois, and as Pastor at St. Agnes Parish in Louisville, Kentucky. He has also worked at the Passionist Retreat Centers in Detroit, Michigan, and Warrenton, Missouri. Presently he resides at the Passionist Retreat Center in Sierra Madre, California, conducts Parish missions and retreats, and assists at the retreat center and at local parishes.

Father Alan accents the positive in his life and in the lives of others. Below Father Alan shares the personal insights and convictions that motivate his positive practices:

> A person's self-image affects his or her ability to hope, dream, dare, and achieve. I seek to encourage and build the self-worth of another through common sense, the teachings of faith, and unconditional acceptance. And I do that in practical ways through my preaching, writing, and photography. I continually assure people of the beauty and goodness of God's creation—especially the human person.

Also by Father Alan:
OUR HEARTS at SUNDAY MASS:
10 Steps to a Joyful Life

To Contact Father Alan:
Fr. Alan Phillip, C.P.
Passionist Community
700 N. Sunnyside Ave.
Sierra Madre, CA 91024-1023
http://www.alanphillipcp.com

ORDER FORM
Alan Phillip, C.P.
Passionists Community Press
700 N. Sunnyside Avenue
Sierra Madre, California 91024-1023
Web: http://www.alanphillipcp.com

DATE:

PURCHASED BY: *(if using credit card use billing address here)*

Name _____
Street _____
City _____ St _____ Zip _____
Phone _____ Email _____

SHIP TO: *(if different from purchaser above)*

Name _____
Street _____
City _____ St _____ Zip _____
Phone _____ Email _____

QTY	TITLE	ISBN	LIST	TOTAL
	OUR HEARTS at SUNDAY MASS: *10 Steps to a Joyful Life* — PAPERBACK	978-1-929753-06-2	$12^{95}	
	FROM BLUES TO SMILES TO JOY: *Practical Steps to a Happier Life!*	978-1-929753-37-6	$14^{95}	
	For more materials by Father Alan visit: http://www.alanphillipcp.com			

DISCOUNTS: available for groups, churches, non-profit orgs, and resale

SPECIAL INSTRUCTIONS/COMMENTS:

SUB-TOTAL	
10% Shipping & Handling	
California Residents Add 8.75% Sales Tax —or— CA Resale Number SR EAA Account #	
TOTAL	

Pay by Credit-Card

PayPal — Credit cards processed on PayPal secure site.
VISA / DISCOVER / BANK
Donations 100% tax-deductible to non-profit account.

CREDIT CARD:
NAME (as it appears on card)
FIRST:_____ M.I._____ LAST: _____
CARD#:_____
CARD HOLDER SIGNATURE:_____

EXPIRATION DATE: _____/_____
SECURITY CODE: _____

Pay by Check—PAYABLE TO: *Alan Phillip, C.P.*

Order Online: http://www.alanphillipcp.com

Order by Phone: 626-355-1740

MAIL TO:
Fr. Alan Phillip, C.P.
Passionist Community
700 N. Sunnyside Ave.
Sierra Madre, CA 91024-1023

Thank You!